11.01
34525
Routledge
Chapman &
Hall

SHELTON STATE LIBRARY

THE CONCISE DICTIONARY OF MANAGEMENT

DISCARDED

THE CONCISE DICTIONARY OF MANAGEMENT

David A. Statt

London and New York

First published 1991
by Routledge
11 New Fetter Lane, London EC4P 4EE

Simultaneously published in the USA and Canada by
Routledge
a division of Routledge, Chapman and Hall Inc.
29 West 35th Street, New York, NY 10001

© 1991 David A. Statt

Typeset by NWL Editorial Services, Langport, Somerset
Printed and bound in Great Britain by
Mackays of Chatham PLC, Chatham, Kent
All rights reserved. No part of this book may be reprinted
or reproduced or utilized in any form or by any electronic,
mechanical, or other means, now known or hereafter
invented, including photocopying and recording, or in any
information storage or retrieval system, without
permission in writing from the publishers.

British Library Cataloguing in Publication Data
Statt, David A. *1942–*
    The concise dictionary of management.
    1. Management
    I. Title
    658

ISBN 0–415–05569–5

Library of Congress Cataloging in Publication Data
has been applied for.

To Judith

ACKNOWLEDGEMENTS

I would like to thank my editor at Routledge, Rosemary Nixon, for her support and encouragement, and my Edinburgh University colleague Gus Napier for his helpful comments on the draft manuscript. Most of all I would like to acknowledge the help of my wife, Judith, the least of whose contributions to this book was the skilled production of an interminably amended manuscript. As some small measure of my gratitude I am delighted to dedicate the book to her.

Edinburgh

A

ability Being able to perform a particular TASK. Implicit in the use of the term is that no further TRAINING is required in order to do so, thus distinguishing it from an APTITUDE.

above the line advertising This is a form of SALES PROMOTION which uses direct advertising through the MASS MEDIA. It is used in opposition to BELOW THE LINE.

absenteeism The absence from WORK of an employee during normal working hours, whether voluntary or involuntary. Voluntary absence is usually considered to be avoidable and without reasonable cause; in effect the employee chooses to be absent. Involuntary absence is usually held to be unavoidable and outwith the employee's control such as unusually difficult weather conditions, breakdown of transport or sickness. A high absenteeism rate is a sign of organizational ill-health in a WORK ORGANIZATION. It is also likely that much of the absenteeism through sickness is job related, either physically in the form of INDUSTRIAL DISEASES or emotionally in the form of PSYCHOSOMATIC DISORDERS.

access time The amount of time taken to retrieve information from the storage facility of a COMPUTER and make it available for use. See also INFORMATION RETRIEVAL.

accident prevention The policy or procedures followed in a workplace to prevent accidents to employees, or at least to reduce the occurrence of accidents. It includes physical aspects like the proper housing of machinery or the provision of protective clothing, and managerial aspects such as effective supervision and TRAINING.

accidents Mishaps that take place at work and may be caused by carelessness, by inadequate safety precautions, or by chance. By law in the United Kingdom accidents causing death or major injury must be reported by the employer or the appropriate authority. Employees are generally entitled to record details of any injuries resulting from accidents in an *accident book* kept at the workplace, and this may be used as evidence for insurance purposes. Some people are thought to be more *accident prone* than others for psychological reasons. While a person's DEPRESSION or unhappiness may decrease their awareness of their surroundings and affect their reactions to a potentially dangerous situation (in anyone at any time) these factors play only a minor role in the incidence of industrial injury.

accountability 1 Being answerable to others for some actions, e.g. to a SUPERVISOR for completing a task or to a board of directors for company PERFORMANCE. 2 Having responsibility and AUTHORITY for seeing that something is carried out as expected, e.g. that sales targets are met or that a BUDGET has been properly spent.

accounting The establishment, maintenance, collection and analysis of financial records. It is used to provide data on the financial position of an ORGANIZATION and any changes that have occurred, or that may occur, over time. This is one aspect of the profession (or art) of accountancy. See also MANAGEMENT ACCOUNTING.

accounting period The length of time between the financial reports produced by an ORGANIZATION. If the reports are for internal use the period is usually either a week or a month; for external information it is usually a year.

achievement A GOAL that has been successfully accomplished. See also NEED FOR ACHIEVEMENT.

acquisitive society A society in which people are constantly encouraged to possess things, e.g. our own. It has been argued by many economists and others that if we didn't have this encouragement our economy would collapse.

action-centred leadership A technique of MANAGEMENT DEVELOPMENT produced in the United Kingdom by John Adair which seeks to provide TRAINING in LEADERSHIP through practical problem-solving. This is an approach to leadership which emphasizes *doing* rather than being and concentrates on the particular behaviour expected of a leader in situations that may vary depending on the needs of the individual, the GROUP and the TASK in hand.

action learning A technique of MANAGEMENT DEVELOPMENT produced in the United Kingdom by R G Revans as an antidote to formal business school methods of TRAINING. As its name implies, this technique focuses on dealing with real and immediate problems, usually within the individual's own ORGANIZATION and usually as part of a GROUP of MANAGERS who contribute different experiences and SKILLS. The individual is thus given the opportunity to learn about GROUP PROCESS and to gain insight into his own behaviour while acquiring practical knowledge and skills.

action research First proposed by KURT LEWIN in the 1930s in his work on GROUP DYNAMICS. The objective of this kind of research is to harness an understanding of the GROUP behaviour being studied to the attempted solution of practical problems within an organizational or social setting. It therefore has both an applied and a theoretical aspect to it, and often includes monitoring and EVALUATION RESEARCH of effectiveness as well.

activities analysis One of three techniques suggested by PETER DRUCKER to help a WORK ORGANIZATION decide on its most appropriate ORGANIZATIONAL STRUCTURE. This technique is to establish what the key activities in the ORGANIZATION actually are as opposed to unquestioned assumptions about what they are. The other two techniques are DECISION ANALYSIS and RELATIONS ANALYSIS.

acuity This term is used in COGNITIVE ERGONOMICS and in ERGONOMICS generally to describe someone's ability to discriminate fine detail in using one of the senses. Most often used of vision, though also used of hearing and other senses.

adaptation Originally a biological term used to describe physical or behavioural changes that increased an organism's chances of survival. Now used in PSYCHOLOGY in two ways: 1 to describe responses to changes in the physical environment, e.g. where the eye adjusts to changes in the light or, 2 where the changed expectations of their society demand some kind of social adaptation in people's behaviour, e.g. the greatly increased number of women at work has led to covert rather than overt DISCRIMINATION against them by men.

adaptive control A form of self-regulation of an industrial process, usually by COMPUTER, where the objective is to maintain a continuous

PERFORMANCE at optimum level through a changing ENVIRONMENT. See also CYBERNETICS.

added value The increase in value of goods or services that results from their PRODUCTION or DISTRIBUTION. It usually involves the transformation of materials by the actions of the work-force. It is often quantified as the difference between revenue from sales and the costs of materials and labour. The term is also used in the PUBLIC SECTOR to indicate intellectual or social gains from a particular INVESTMENT compared to other uses of the same funds, e.g. the gains in understanding of a social issue from the work of a research centre as opposed to the work of isolated individuals scattered throughout the country.

adhocracy A NEOLOGISM introduced by Alvin Toffler (who also invented FUTURE SHOCK). It refers to the tendency in an ORGANIZATION to progress on the basis of temporary, *ad hoc* GROUPS, such as a TASK FORCE, brought together to deal with a particular project only.

administration 1 The CONTROL, direction, or MANAGEMENT of an ORGANIZATION. 2 The group of people who have the responsibility for these functions. Used especially in the PUBLIC SECTOR.

administrative management theory An approach to the study of MANAGEMENT, based on the work of HENRI FAYOL and others in the 1930s, which emphasizes the importance of the formal structure and the HIERARCHY of an ORGANIZATION.

administrative science The systematic study of ADMINISTRATION in all its aspects. It includes both BUSINESS ADMINISTRATION and PUBLIC ADMINISTRATION and attempts to formulate general principles that are applicable to all forms of ORGANIZATION.

ADP See AUTOMATIC DATA PROCESSING

adrenalin A hormone secreted by the adrenal glands (which are situated on top of the kidneys) in times of excitement or STRESS. It increases the heart rate, the blood supply, the sugar supply from the liver into the blood stream and alerts the muscles to impulses from the nervous system, thereby preparing the body for action. If the body is in a WORK situation and unable to take any physical action the resulting frustration can contribute to a variety of PSYCHOSOMATIC DISORDERS.

advertising The publicizing, PROMOTION and COMMUNICATION of information or opinions about a product or service, or even an

ORGANIZATION, to a potential MARKET. The means used may be ABOVE THE LINE or BELOW THE LINE.

affirmative action   An American term used to describe the provision of opportunities for disadvantaged groups by paying particular attention to the RECRUITMENT, TRAINING and PROMOTION of people who have been subject to DISCRIMINATION in EMPLOYMENT practices.

ageism   DISCRIMINATION against older people, eg, ORGANIZATIONS reluctant to hire secretaries over forty, or models over twenty. Like RACISM and SEXISM this is based on an attribute arbitrarily determined by birth – in this case age.

AI   See ARTIFICIAL INTELLIGENCE.

alcoholism   A condition in which someone is dependent on alcohol and drinks excessive amounts of it. A widespread, if rarely discussed, problem in the workplace.

algorithm   A set of rules to be used in solving a problem. It usually takes the form of a fixed procedure with a logical sequence of steps. Extensively used in COMPUTER PROGRAMS and SYSTEMS ANALYSIS.

ALGOL (Algorithmic Language)   A SYSTEM of words and symbols used in science and TECHNOLOGY to instruct a COMPUTER in its TASK of INFORMATION PROCESSING. See COMPUTER LANGUAGE.

alienation   A term with various shades of meaning in PSYCHOLOGY and SOCIOLOGY all of which refer in common to feelings of being estranged, separated, and powerless, whether in relation to oneself, to WORK, to nature, to other people, to wealth and the means of PRODUCTION in a society, or else to society as a whole.

allocation   1 The process of dividing resources or costs between different sections or functions of an ORGANIZATION. 2 The amount of resources in a given BUDGET.

alternating shift   A two-shift system of working in which, for example, people may WORK days and then nights for the same period of time, often week and week about, or perhaps alternating early and late shifts.

analysis of variance   In STATISTICS this is a technique for determining whether there is a relationship between several sets of data. It involves examining the VARIANCE between MEANS on different data sets to see whether it exceeds what would be expected by chance alone. If the means are sufficiently close a relationship is presumed.

annual report An account of an ORGANIZATION's activities over a twelve-month period, drawn up by its MANAGEMENT. Required by law for registered companies. It may include an ACCOUNTING of HUMAN RESOURCES as well as financial resources.

anomie A term used by the French sociologist Emile Durkheim to describe a condition of society where SOCIAL NORMS are breaking down and people may become confused both about their place in society and about their sense of IDENTITY. This may lead them to suffer a form of ALIENATION.

ANOVA See ANALYSIS OF VARIANCE.

anthropology The study of the different physical and cultural conditions of humankind.

anthropometry A branch of ANTHROPOLOGY that is concerned with measuring human physical characteristics. It is used in a workplace ENVIRONMENT when the nature of human size, shape and movement are of particular concern.

anticipatory socialization Where someone is eager to enter a new ROLE, they may anticipate the situation by adopting the ATTITUDES and interests associated with it, e.g. someone about to become a student, or a MANAGER, or a parent for the first time. See also SOCIALIZATION and PROFESSIONAL SOCIALIZATION.

anxiety A term used with many shades of meaning and in many different areas of PSYCHOLOGY. It is generally held to be an unpleasant emotional state resulting from STRESS or CONFLICT, and characterized by fear and apprehension. Everyone suffers from anxiety at some time and some situations would make virtually everyone anxious. But if the fear and apprehension felt are vague and diffuse and not attached to a specific object, or if they seem excessive, the anxiety is considered to be a neurotic TRAIT of the individual's PERSONALITY.

applied psychology The term normally used for those areas of PSYCHOLOGY which attempt to apply psychological theories and findings to particular issues of everyday life, such as COUNSELLING, education or INDUSTRIAL RELATIONS. It can also be used to describe the contributions of psychologists in a wide variety of more unusual areas such as designing instrument panels for spaceships and assisting police in dealing with hostage takers.

appraisal interview See PERFORMANCE APPRAISAL INTERVIEW.

apprenticeship The period of time spent, mostly at the workplace and usually on low wages, in learning the basic SKILLS of a craft, trade or profession.

appropriation Money allocated to a BUDGET for a specific purpose.

aptitude The potential for acquiring a SKILL or ABILITY after some TRAINING.

aptitude test A technique that tries to predict a person's capacity for acquiring a certain SKILL or ABILITY. See also PSYCHOMETRICS.

arbitration A method of settling a dispute between two parties who have failed to agree on some matter. With the agreement of both parties to abide by the arbiter's decision the dispute is put before a neutral third party, usually an independent body, for adjudication outside a court of law.

Argyris, Chris (born 1923) An American psychologist and specialist in ORGANIZATIONAL DEVELOPMENT whose work focuses on the relationship between the individual and the ORGANIZATION, and in particular the search for conditions that foster the integration of individual needs and ORGANIZATIONAL GOALS.

Army Alpha Test The earliest example of a PAPER-AND-PENCIL TEST used by a large ORGANIZATION in the RECRUITMENT, SELECTION and PLACEMENT of very large numbers of people. This was a test of INTELLIGENCE used by the United States army to screen new recruits during the first World War.

artificial intelligence A field of study, combining PSYCHOLOGY and INFORMATION TECHNOLOGY, which uses COMPUTER SYSTEMS to develop machines that exhibit characteristics of human INTELLIGENCE, like language and problem-solving. These machines are intended to reproduce human thought processes and are used especially in the development of EXPERT SYSTEMS which simulate human expertise, e.g. bank managers making loan decisions or doctors making diagnoses of patients.

Asch, Solomon (born 1907) An American psychologist, influenced by the GESTALT viewpoint, who has specialized in the study of CONFORMITY behaviour in small GROUPS. His most important contribution to GROUP DYNAMICS is considered to be the finding that some people can be persuaded to doubt the evidence of their own eyes by the force of group pressure. (Fig. 1)

assembly line

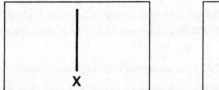

Figure 1 Asch conformity situation

assembly line A means of MASS PRODUCTION, based on the ideas of GILBRETH and TAYLOR, which was invented by HENRY FORD in 1913 for his model-T car factory. It quickly became the leading method of producing standardized goods in large volumes. The method requires each worker to carry out his particular task on the product as it passes in front of him along a conveyor belt, each worker adding something to the product along the way. A TASK may take as little as a couple of seconds to perform and the possible psychological effects of doing this all day long have been explored by the well-known psychologist C. Chaplin in his film *Modern Times*. See also AUTONOMOUS WORK GROUPS and DEPERSONALIZATION.

assertiveness training A form of TRAINING designed to increase a person's confidence. It uses a technique of BEHAVIOUR MODIFICATION intended to help people overcome INHIBITIONS about expressing their feelings. This technique involves a lot of ROLE PLAYING. It is quite often used in MANAGEMENT DEVELOPMENT.

assessment 1 A procedure to identify ABILITY carried out on individuals as part of the processes of RECRUITMENT and SELECTION. 2 A procedure carried out on property or PROFITS to determine tax liability.

assessment centre An establishment, often set up within large ORGANIZATIONS, that specializes in identifying ABILITY, as part of the processes of RECRUITMENT and SELECTION and identifying potential for MANAGEMENT DEVELOPMENT. See also CAREER DEVELOPMENT.

asset stripping The acquisition of an ORGANIZATION for the sole purpose of selling off its most valuable ASSETS in order to make a quick PROFIT.

assets Resources an ORGANIZATION owns which are of economic benefit to it. These may be tangible (like machinery or property) or intangible (like GOODWILL).

association A GROUP of people or ORGANIZATIONS sharing the same interest who wish to be affiliated with each other. This affiliation may be formal or informal; highly organized or loosely structured; world-wide in scope or restricted to a single building.

attitude A stable, long-lasting, and learned predisposition to respond to certain things in a certain way. An attitude has three aspects to it: belief, feeling and action.

attitude scale A set of questions designed to elicit ATTITUDES and measure their strength.

attitude survey The use of SURVEY RESEARCH to obtain information on ATTITUDES.

audioconferencing A TELECONFERENCE using only audio means of COMMUNICATION.

audiovisual aids Techniques making use of hearing and (especially) vision that are used in order to improve COMMUNICATION. They range from blackboard and chalk to COMPUTER ASSISTED INSTRUCTION in complexity – though not necessarily in effectiveness.

audit 1 The process of verifying the ACCOUNTING records of an ORGANIZATION by an independent auditor to see whether they contain a true, fair and accurate account of business transacted. 2 The term may also be used in relation to HUMAN RESOURCES, as in MANAGEMENT AUDIT.

authoritarian management A type of MANAGEMENT which emphasizes the discipline and control of people and sees little value in consulting them about the JOB. What you would expect from an AUTHORITARIAN PERSONALITY. It is usually contrasted with DEMOCRATIC MANAGEMENT.

authoritarian personality A person characterized by a concern with obedience and various TRAITS that seem to be associated with it, such as low TOLERANCE FOR AMBIGUITY, high PREJUDICE, rigid adherence to conventions, superstition, servility and contempt for weakness.

authority 1 The right, inherent in a job or function, to use POWER in the fulfilment of one's responsibilities. Power and authority do not always go together, of course. People in positions of authority may be ineffective in using power because they do not command the respect or loyalty of their subordinates, and people with no official authority may exert a powerful effect on an ORGANIZATION by virtue of their personal qualities, their long experience, or the fact that they married the boss's daughter. 2 The term is also used of a public body with statutory powers and responsibilities, such as a Local Authority.

Automatic Data Processing See ELECTRONIC DATA PROCESSING.

automation A term first used in the late 1940s by the Ford Motor Company. It is used to describe the employment of machines that reduce or dispense entirely with HUMAN COMMUNICATION, computation or CONTROL in relation to a JOB. It is particularly important in INFORMATION PROCESSING and INTELLIGENT KNOWLEDGE-BASED SYSTEMS.

autonomous work groups A form of WORK ORGANIZATION where workers have the opportunity and the responsibility for planning and carrying out their TASKS without the direct supervision of MANAGEMENT. It is thought to increase JOB SATISFACTION and possibly also PRODUCTIVITY and is in direct opposition to the idea of the ASSEMBLY LINE.

autonomy Independence or self-determination either for individuals or for ORGANIZATIONS. Often a matter of degree rather than an absolute condition.

B

balance of payments The difference between the payments a country makes to other countries and those it receives, over a certain period of time.

banding A way of organizing a SALARY STRUCTURE where a series of different levels are first established into which jobs are then classified by level, or band, rather than fixing a different rate of PAY for each job individually.

bandwidth 1 A term used in the FLEXIBLE WORKING HOURS system to describe the total working day of an ORGANIZATION from the earliest permitted starting time to the latest permitted finishing time. 2 A term used in TELECOMMUNICATIONS for the frequency limits to a given communications band.

bar chart A graphical method of illustrating statistical information. It takes the form of a diagram in which quantities or frequencies are

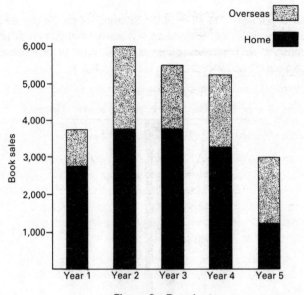

Figure 2 Bar chart

expressed as columns of different height. See also GANTT CHART and HISTOGRAM. (Fig. 2)

bargaining 1 A term used in INDUSTRIAL RELATIONS to describe negotiations between two parties, usually employers and employees or their representatives, to achieve a settlement regarding wages and conditions of EMPLOYMENT. 2 The kind of behaviour studied in various areas of SOCIAL PSYCHOLOGY, especially GAME THEORY, where people with different interests try to influence each other in order to improve their position. 3 Transacting business on the stock exchange.

BASIC An introductory COMPUTER LANGUAGE that combines ALGOL, COBOL and FORTRAN.

batch production A type of PRODUCTION different from MASS PRODUCTION or CONTINUOUS PROCESS PRODUCTION in that it is used where identical items are to be manufactured and processed in groups, or batches, rather than individually, e.g. gloves, toolkits or matching lingerie.

behaviour modification The deliberate changing of a particular pattern of behaviour (eg. increased smoking or drinking in times of STRESS) by using methods based on the theory of BEHAVIOURISM.

11

behavioural science The study of the behaviour of people and animals by use of experiment and observation. It is centred around PSYCHOLOGY but branches out towards biology and physiology in one direction, ANTHROPOLOGY and SOCIOLOGY in the other. (Fig. 3)

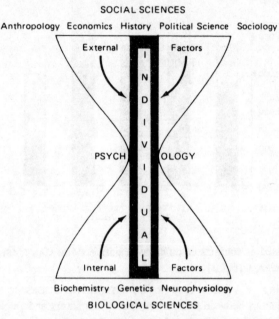

Figure 3 Behavioural science

behavioural theory of the firm A concept proposed in the early 1960s by two American psychologists, Richard Cyert and James March, which argues that an ORGANIZATION consists of a coalition of different interest groups with different GOALS representing a variety of views and continuously BARGAINING for POWER. This means that decision making is an inherently uncertain business – contrary to the assumptions of rational behaviour made by proponents of CLASSICAL ORGANIZATION THEORY or ECONOMIC MAN.

Behaviourism A school of PSYCHOLOGY founded by an American psychologist, J B WATSON, in 1913. Watson believed that the work of PAVLOV on CONDITIONING represented the future of PSYCHOLOGY, which should deal solely with the objective study of human and animal behaviour and eschew 'woolly' concepts like mind and consciousness. Watson is now generally regarded as much too extreme and simple-minded, having been superseded by B F SKINNER and others. For cultural and historical reasons BEHAVIOURISM has continued to flourish more in the United States than elsewhere. Watson himself left academia to pursue a successful career in ADVERTISING with the J Walter Thompson Company.

bell-shaped curve This describes the shape of the curve obtained by plotting the kind of FREQUENCY DISTRIBUTION known as a NORMAL DISTRIBUTION on a graph.

below the line advertising This is a form of SALES PROMOTION which uses outlets such as direct mail, special discounts and point-of-sale offers as opposed to the MASS MEDIA used in ABOVE THE LINE ADVERTISING.

benefit in kind Any payment for WORK performed other than money. The most common example is the company car. See also BLACK ECONOMY, FRINGE BENEFIT and PERK.

bimodal distribution A FREQUENCY DISTRIBUTION that has two MODES.

bio-data See BIOGRAPHICAL DATA.

biofeedback The FEEDBACK of information to individuals about their biological functions. Using biofeedback it is possible for people to gain a certain amount of CONTROL of such functions as heart rate, blood pressure and brain waves through a form of CONDITIONING process.

biographical data The kind of personal information recorded in a CURRICULUM VITAE. It is used in the RECRUITMENT and SELECTION of applicants for jobs.

biological clock Not a physical structure but a term used to describe the biochemical mechanism that controls our BIORHYTHMS.

biorhythms Biological systems that have regularly recurring cycles. The best known of these are the menstrual cycle, and the CIRCADIAN RHYTHMS which are of particular interest to psychologists.

biosocial The interaction of biological and social factors in the study of society, e.g. the social effects of birth-rate or HIV infection.

biotechnology The use of biologically-based processes in existing manu-facturing and service industries.

black-coated workers A sartorial alternative to WHITE-COLLAR WORKERS.

black economy The widely-used name for the set of informal economic activities, engaged in outside the official systems of EMPLOYMENT and TAXATION, on which no documents are kept and no tax paid. PAYMENT IN KIND or cash is the usual procedure. The people involved in this activity may well be regularly employed and perhaps MOONLIGHTING on the side.

black market An illegal trade in goods or services the demand for which has outstripped the officially available supply. It is caused by the imposition of official measures designed to cope with the shortfall, like rationing or price controls.

blackleg A derogatory term (origin unknown) used to describe someone who does not support the INDUSTRIAL ACTION of his fellow workers and, for example, continues to work during a STRIKE or replaces a striking worker.

blacklist A list of people or ORGANIZATIONS against whom some kind of DISCRIMINATION will be practised, usually for political reasons.

Blau typology A technique used by the American sociologist Peter Blau which classifies FORMAL ORGANIZATIONS according to the criterion 'who benefits'? Four classes of ORGANIZATION are thereby distinguished: 1 *Mutual-benefit associations*, like clubs and political parties, 2 *Business concerns*, like banks and shops, 3 *Service organizations*, like hospitals and schools, 4 *Commonweal organizations*, like the fire and police services.

blind test A technique used in MARKET RESEARCH for obtaining the opinions of consumers on a product where all of the product's identifying marks are removed. Several products are sometimes compared at the same time in this fashion.

blue chip 1 The term used to describe the ordinary shares of long-established, large and reputable companies. Such shares are generally regarded as being a good long-term INVESTMENT. 2 More generally the term may be used of anything that is highly regarded for its reliability and PERFORMANCE.

blue-collar worker Popular term for a MANUAL WORKER in a factory or other industrial workplace. The name derives from the typical shirts or overalls worn. Usually contrasted with a WHITE-COLLAR WORKER.

body language NON-VERBAL COMMUNICATION with other people by means of physical postures, movements, or gestures that may be conscious or UNCONSCIOUS on the part of the communicator.

body-shopping A term sometimes used of the practice whereby a

CONSULTANCY supplies people to work on a temporary contract basis in place of regular STAFF in the PUBLIC SECTOR.

bookkeeping The method of recording an ORGANIZATION's financial transactions that allows a clear picture of its financial situation to be obtained at any time, i.e. by reference to its 'books'. See also DOUBLE-ENTRY BOOKKEEPING.

boomerang effect A term used in SOCIAL PSYCHOLOGY, in the study of attitude change. It refers to someone who changes her ATTITUDE in the opposite direction from that being advocated to her.

brainstorming In SOCIAL PSYCHOLOGY this term refers to the free generation of ideas by the members of a GROUP for the purpose of solving a specific problem.

brand A mark, name, LOGO or TRADEMARK that identifies a product or service or ORGANIZATION and distinguishes it from its competitors.

brand leader A term used in MARKETING to describe a BRAND or a product that appears to be the most prominent one in its field to consumers, and is marketed accordingly – unlike a follower in the MARKET or a new product.

brand loyalty A situation where consumers remain loyal to a particular BRAND of goods or services even if it costs more than its competitors.

branding The use of a BRAND to describe a product, service or ORGANIZATION. At its most successful it becomes a generic term for its whole field, e.g. the use of 'Xerox' for photocopiers.

break-even point The point in an ORGANIZATION's financial life where its INCOME equals its costs.

brightness A term used in ERGONOMICS to describe both the objective intensity of the physical stimulus from a source of light and the subjective sensation of the person who experiences it.

buddy system The American equivalent of SITTING NEXT TO NELLIE.

budget 1 The financial statement of an ORGANIZATION's planned INCOME and expenditure for a given length of time. 2 The proposed income and expenditure of the British government over the coming year as presented to Parliament by the Chancellor of the Exchequer. 3 Sometimes used in place of APPROPRIATION.

budget-based institution An ORGANIZATION that is required to prepare, and work to, a BUDGET.

bug An error or fault in the SOFTWARE which causes a COMPUTER PROGRAM to malfunction.

built-in obsolescence The deliberate design of a product so that it needs replacing after a certain length of time.

bureaucracy 1 A term coined by the German sociologist Max Weber in the late nineteenth century to describe an ORGANIZATION that has (a) a clearly-defined HIERARCHY with top-down AUTHORITARIAN MANAGE-MENT, (b) highly-specialized responsibilities, ROLES and TASKS for its members, (c) a heavy emphasis on rules and procedures. Though these characteristics are mainly associated with large organizations they are found to some extent in all organizations. 2 'The bureaucracy' is a term sometimes used in the PUBLIC SECTOR to describe the civil service.

burnout A term used to describe people at WORK who have suffered from the effects of STRESS to the point where they are overloaded and no longer able to function productively. People in this situation may become cynical and just go through the motions if the source of stress is not dealt with. See also RETIREMENT ON THE JOB.

business administration This term usually refers to the field of study concerned with the CONTROL, direction, or MANAGEMENT of a business ORGANIZATION.

business game A form of TRAINING for MANAGEMENT where the elements of a business situation are presented to the trainees who then have to make decisions about how best to manage the situation. It involves ROLE PLAYING, is usually done in a group, sometimes competitively, and increasingly with the aid of COMPUTER SIMULATION.

business plan See CORPORATE PLAN.

busy-work The American version of MAKE-WORK.

buyer's market A MARKET situation in which buyers have more POWER to influence prices and conditions of sale than sellers, usually because supply exceeds demand. Always contrasted with SELLER'S MARKET.

buying-in The practice of hiring expert help as required by an ORGANIZATION rather then employing such experts on its STAFF.

C

CAD See COMPUTER-AIDED DESIGN.

CAD/CAM system An integrated SYSTEM used in INDUSTRIAL ENGIN-EERING that employs both COMPUTER-AIDED DESIGN and COMPUTER-AIDED MANUFACTURING.

CAE See COMPUTER-AIDED ENGINEERING.

CAI See COMPUTER-ASSISTED INSTRUCTION.

CAM See COMPUTER-AIDED MANUFACTURING.

capital 1 In ACCOUNTING, capital is the term for the total financial ASSETS of an ORGANIZATION whether in the form of money, property, goods or equipment. It represents the organization's stock of wealth as opposed to its INCOME. The organization's HUMAN RESOURCES may be represented in the form of HUMAN ASSET ACCOUNTING. 2 In ECONOMICS, capital is traditionally one of the three major factors necessary for PRODUCTION along with labour and land.

capital-intensive The term used of an ORGANIZATION with a relatively high degree of CAPITAL invested in AUTOMATION as opposed to people, e.g. a car manufacturer. It is therefore the opposite of LABOUR-INTENSIVE.

capitalism An economic SYSTEM characterized by the private ownership of a society's resources; by COMPETITION in the pursuit of financial gain; and by support for the ideal of a FREE MARKET in goods and services.

career A line of WORK that a person expects to pursue for his or her foreseeable working life, and one that might include changes in JOB or employer.

career anchors A concept developed by the American theorist of ORGANIZATIONAL PSYCHOLOGY, Edgar Schein, to study the guidelines and priorities in the working life of a MANAGER. It deals with the way in which a person's SELF-IMAGE focuses around their needs, motives, talents and values and the clarification of what is most important to them, such as the use of technical SKILLS or finding stability or security in an ORGANIZATION.

career development The planning of a person's future CAREER in an

ORGANIZATION in order to maximize their contribution to the organization and the fulfilment of their own potential. A primary function of PERSONNEL MANAGEMENT. See also ROLE and WORK.

career expectations The rewards that a person expects from his or her future CAREER.

career goals The ACHIEVEMENT targets that people aim for in a CAREER.

career ladders Recognized routes of PROMOTION and advancement in an ORGANIZATION.

career patterns The identification of regularities or typical paths through an ORGANIZATION that show up in people's CAREERS.

cartel A combination of two or more independent ORGANIZATIONS which produce the same product, for the purposes of eliminating or restricting COMPETITION between them and preventing new competitors from entering the MARKET. This is accomplished by fixing prices, level of PRODUCTION, or MARKET SEGMENTATION, e.g. the Organization of Petroleum Exporting Countries (OPEC).

case studies A form of TRAINING for MANAGEMENT used extensively to develop SKILLS of analysis, reasoning and judgement. It is based mainly on real-life situations. Case studies are associated particularly with the teaching methods of the Harvard Business School. Unlike BUSINESS GAMES they have no action component.

cash flow 1 The amount of cash flowing into and out of an ORGANIZATION. 2 The amount of cash required to finance operating expenses or further PRODUCTION over a given period of time.

caveat emptor Latin for 'let the buyer beware', and used to indicate the widely held legal principle that the onus is on the buyer, in the first instance, to check that he or she is getting the goods or services paid for.

CBA See COST-BENEFIT ANALYSIS.

CBT See COMPUTER-BASED TRAINING.

cell organization A form of WORK ORGANIZATION that groups together workers concerned with the various activities of one part of a manufacturing process into a 'cell'. Often used in BATCH PRODUCTION.

central bank Usually a government's own bank, like the Bank of England or the Federal Reserve Bank in the United States, which carries out the government's financial policy. It also oversees the operation of a country's financial SYSTEM, acting as banker to the other banks.

centralization The policy and process of trying to run everything in an ORGANIZATION from one central point.

certification The process of obtaining an official document to satisfy some institutional requirement. Most often used in the field of education or TRAINING or the provision of professional services.

chain of command The arrangement by which instructions and information are passed down through the HIERARCHY of LINE MANAGEMENT in an ORGANIZATION.

chairman's brief A document written by the SECRETARY of an ORGANIZATION or COMMITTEE in the PUBLIC SECTOR to prepare the committee chairman for a forthcoming meeting.

change agent A person who acts as a catalyst within an ORGANIZATION to assist the introduction, implementation or facilitation of changes as a result of an ORGANIZATIONAL DEVELOPMENT programme.

chargehand The leading member of a WORK GROUP under the supervision of a FOREMAN.

charisma An elusive quality of PERSONALITY, often defined as 'personal magnetism', which is widely considered to be an important element in LEADERSHIP, especially TRANSFORMATIONAL LEADERSHIP.

charm price An alternative term for PSYCHOLOGICAL PRICE.

chart A diagrammatic way of expressing information, e.g. BAR CHART, HISTOGRAM, PICTOGRAM and PIE CHART.

chi square In STATISTICS this is a simple TEST, represented by the Greek letter chi (χ), which is widely used in research in PSYCHOLOGY and the BEHAVIOURAL SCIENCES to see whether observed results differ from those expected by chance alone.

chief executive The most senior EXECUTIVE officer of an ORGANIZATION, e.g. the permanent SECRETARY of a government department or the president of an American corporation.

chip A shortened, colloquial form of MICROCHIP.

chronobiology The study of BIORHYTHMS.

chunking The process of grouping items of information into units, or 'chunks', as an aid to memorizing them.

CIM See COMPUTER INTEGRATED MANUFACTURING.

circadian rhythm The term circadian, from the Latin meaning 'about a day' refers to those BIORHYTHMS which function on roughly a 24-hour cycle, like sleeping, and changes in blood pressure and body temperature.

CIT See CRITICAL INCIDENT TECHNIQUE.

classical organization theory The attempt, in the early years of the twentieth century, to formulate a set of general principles of ADMINISTRATION that would serve as a guide to the effective MANAGEMENT of any ORGANIZATION. It is associated with the work of FAYOL and TAYLOR amongst others.

clinical psychology The branch of psychology concerned with the application of psychological theory and research to the diagnosis and treatment of emotional, mental or behavioural disorders.

clique An INFORMAL GROUP whose members associate with each other at WORK (as in society generally) on the basis of mutual interests or just physical proximity. In SOCIOLOGY the term does not have quite the pejorative connotation of in-group exclusiveness that it has in popular usage.

closed shop A situation in which all the members of an ORGANIZATION must belong to the appropriate TRADE UNION. After legislation passed in the 1980s this is no longer formally possible in the United Kingdom.

closure 1 A GESTALT principle, generally accepted in PSYCHOLOGY, that the brain has a built-in tendency to perceive meaning, completion, and coherence where the objective sensory facts may have no meaning, be incomplete, or incoherent. Thus a figure with a part missing will be perceived as though it were whole. (Fig. 4) 2 The term is also used in PSYCHO-

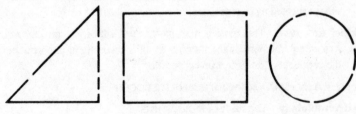

Figure 4 Closure

THERAPY (and even in general parlance) to denote a line of investigation that is being brought to completion. **3** A related usage is that of 'closing' a deal.

cluster sampling A term used in MARKET RESEARCH for the practice of drawing a sample of informants from a geographically localized area (like a single street) – a much cheaper procedure than RANDOM SAMPLING or even QUOTA SAMPLING.

CNC machines Machines that are under COMPUTER NUMERICAL CONTROL.

co-opting Inviting someone to join an already established GROUP because of some particular QUALITY or SKILL, the need for which may not have been foreseen when the group was set up.

co-ordination The process of integrating all the parts and functions of an ORGANIZATION.

coacting group A term used in SOCIOLOGY for people who share the same GOAL but WORK towards it by themselves, without any interaction or COMMUNICATION. A form of PLURALISTIC IGNORANCE perhaps.

COBOL (Common Business Oriented Language) A SYSTEM of words and symbols used in business to instruct a COMPUTER in its TASK of INFORMATION PROCESSING. See COMPUTER LANGUAGE.

coefficient See CORRELATION COEFFICIENT.

coercion The use of POWER to get people to do something they would not otherwise do. Typical of AUTHORITARIAN MANAGEMENT.

cognition A general term which includes all the psychological processes by which people become aware of, and gain knowledge about, the world.

cognitive dissonance A theory developed in SOCIAL PSYCHOLOGY by the American psychologist Leon Festinger. The theory states that because we have a powerful DRIVE towards consistency (or consonance), if we hold two *psychologically* inconsistent COGNITIONS (beliefs, ATTITUDES, values or ideas) at the same time, or if our behaviour clashes with those cognitions, we will be in an unpleasant state of tension which we are strongly motivated to reduce. As the theory deals with psychological rather than logical inconsistency it proposes that we are not so much concerned with actually being consistent as with *feeling that we are* consistent.

cognitive ergonomics A form of ERGONOMICS in which factors of COGNITION are more important than physical factors.

cohort effect A cohort is generally defined as a GROUP of people who have lived through a certain period of time and shared common historical experiences, like the Second World War or the advent of television. It is used in particular of people born in the same year. It is thought that cohorts born several decades apart, for instance, may be affected in systematically different ways by the different ZEITGEIST and social/ environmental conditions of their times.

cold calling A form of selling where the salesman approaches a prospective customer – by telephone, by post, or in person – with no prior contact being made.

collective bargaining An INDUSTRIAL RELATIONS process in which employers or their representatives negotiate with employees or their (TRADE UNION) representatives on the level of WAGES and the conditions of EMPLOYMENT for a GROUP of employees as a whole, rather than for individuals.

colour blindness A total or partial inability to distinguish colours. Total colour blindness is very rare but partial colour blindness (particularly the inability to distinguish red and green from each other or from grey) is surprisingly common. It has been estimated that about 8 to 10 per cent of males are born with this defect, though it is rare in females. Of relevance to ERGONOMICS.

command economy See PLANNED ECONOMY.

committee A GROUP of people appointed by an ORGANIZATION to take responsibility for a particular TASK or function on behalf of the organization as a whole. The committee may or may not be given EXECUTIVE power. It may be a permanent standing committee or a temporary *ad hoc* committee.

communication The process of transmitting or exchanging information, ideas, beliefs and opinions, mainly by the use of language – though NON-VERBAL COMMUNICATION can also be important in certain situations. Transmission of information may be by FORMAL COMMUNICATION or INFORMAL COMMUNICATION. See also CHAIN OF COMMAND, COMMUNICATION NETWORKS, INFORMATION THEORY, INFORMATION TECHNOLOGY and SOCIAL DISTANCE.

communication network A method or form or pattern of

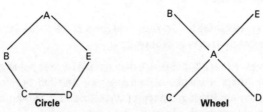

Figure 5 Communication network

COMMUNICATION. The two most frequently studied kinds of networks are wheel-shaped and circle-shaped. The wheel network facilitates quick and accurate communication but is less equipped to handle complexity and change. The circle network adapts well to complexity and change in communication and seems to involve and satisfy its members better. These networks are often discussed in the comparison of a MECHANISTIC ORGANIZATION and an ORGANIC ORGANIZATION. (Fig. 5)

communication theory   See INFORMATION THEORY.

communicator credibility   In SOCIAL PSYCHOLOGY this term describes the extent to which the communicator of a message is believable. It is thought to be related to whether the communicator is perceived as expert and trustworthy or not.

company town   A town dominated by a single employer. Such towns are usually small, but there are exceptions. Washington DC is sometimes described as a company town, the 'company' in this case being the United States government.

company union   An employer's version of a TRADE UNION within a single ORGANIZATION. It does not have the independent STATUS or POWER to represent the employees in any INDUSTRIAL RELATIONS matters.

compatibility   1 People being able to work together. 2 Machines and units of TECHNOLOGY being able to work together.

compensation   1 Payment for injury, damage or loss. 2 The term is also used, particularly in the United States, for the remuneration of salary and FRINGE BENEFITS.

competition   The attempt to do better than others supplying goods and services in the same MARKET. Fostering competition is one of the basic principles of CAPITALISM, which was first formulated in the eighteenth century by ADAM SMITH.

competitive advantage Anything that gives an ORGANIZATION an edge over the COMPETITION in its MARKET.

compliance 1 In SOCIAL PSYCHOLOGY this is a form of yielding to GROUP pressure where a change of behaviour is exhibited by someone but without any underlying change of ATTITUDE. 2 Obeying a statutory requirement or a legal obligation.

comptroller Traditional form of the term CONTROLLER, from the French verb *comptroller*, to check off.

compulsion 1 An overwhelming UNCONSCIOUS need to engage in some behaviour that is usually contrary to one's conscious wishes. 2 Being made to obey a statutory requirement or a legal obligation.

computer An electronic machine for processing information automatically and very quickly.

Computer-aided Design A process in which a designer interacts with a COMPUTER SYSTEM to produce a design, from the original idea to the finished product, by electronic manipulation and the use of a VISUAL DISPLAY UNIT rather than pencil and paper. Closely associated with COMPUTER AIDED MANUFACTURING.

Computer-aided Engineering The process that links COMPUTER-AIDED DESIGN with COMPUTER-AIDED MANUFACTURING, for example in the manufacture of tools or machines under COMPUTER NUMERICAL CONTROL.

Computer-aided Manufacturing COMPUTERIZATION of all the steps in the manufacture of a product.

Computer-assisted Instruction A method of PROGRAMMED LEARNING in which a computer is used as a TEACHING MACHINE.

Computer-based Practice A method of learning in which the medium of instruction is the COMPUTER or COMPUTER TERMINAL.

Computer-based Training A method of TRAINING in which the medium of instruction, with which the individual interacts, is the COMPUTER or COMPUTER TERMINAL.

computer graphics Pictorial images displayed on a Visual Display Unit and generated by use of a COMPUTER.

Computer-integrated Manufacturing The ultimate form of AUTOMATION in which every aspect of manufacturing, from the initial design to the delivery of the finished product, is both controlled and co-ordinated by COMPUTER.

computer language A SYSTEM of words and symbols used to instruct a COMPUTER in its TASK of INFORMATION PROCESSING. The most popular computer language in business is COBOL (Common Business Oriented Language); in science and TECHNOLOGY ALGOL (Algorithmic Language) and FORTRAN (Formula Translation) are commonly used. An introductory computer language that combines aspects of all three is called BASIC.

computer literacy The ABILITY to use COMPUTER LANGUAGE.

Computer Numerical Control The control of machines by COMPUTER using numerical information.

computer package This refers to the SOFTWARE required for a particular application.

computer program A set of instructions to a COMPUTER, written in a COMPUTER LANGUAGE, that tells it to perform a particular task. The spelling of 'PROGRAM' is usually American, in recognition of the American predominance in this field.

computer simulation A SIMULATION exercise conducted by COMPUTER, e.g. to produce the realistic experience of flying in the TRAINING of airline pilots.

computer terminal A machine linked to a COMPUTER, however remote, and having access to all its data.

computerization The installation of computers as part of a process of AUTOMATION.

conditioning A process of LEARNING in humans or animals, via an experimental procedure using REINFORCEMENT, where a given stimulus produces a response other than its normal, natural or automatic one. In the classical form developed by PAVLOV a dog learned to salivate at the sound of a bell and not just when its food was presented. B F SKINNER developed a procedure called operant conditioning in which an animal's simple response could be used as the basis for TRAINING it to engage in very complex behaviour, like circus tricks. Humans can be trained to control bodily processes like blood pressure or brain waves.

conflict A situation in which there are mutually antagonistic interests, needs, or motives involving individuals or GROUPS. The most easily recognized indicator of conflict in a WORK ORGANIZATION is a STRIKE but a lot of conflict may be unspoken, or even UNCONSCIOUS, and is very difficult for organizations to handle.

conflict management The conscious attempt to identify CONFLICT within an ORGANIZATION and to deal with it in such a way that its potential for disruption is neutralized.

conflict resolution The conscious attempt to identify CONFLICT within an ORGANIZATION and to deal with it in such a way that it disappears. Much more ambitious, and much rarer, than CONFLICT MANAGEMENT.

conformity The tendency to allow one's ATTITUDES, opinions, perceptions and behaviour to be influenced by others. This may be due to a deep-lying TRAIT of someone's PERSONALITY or to the kind of GROUP pressures that would lead most people to conform. This area is an important part of SOCIAL PSYCHOLOGY, to which leading contributions have been made by ASCH and MILGRAM amongst others.

conglomerate A business ORGANIZATION, usually comprising a group of companies, with diverse and often unrelated financial interests but sometimes trading under the one name.

consensual validation Checking one's perceptions of something with other people as a way of knowing whether what is perceived is real or illusory. The psychological basis of the ASCH experiments on CONFORMITY.

construct validity The extent to which each item of a PSYCHOLOGICAL TEST measures or predicts what it's supposed to.

constructive dismissal The legal term for a situation in which an employee leaves an ORGANIZATION, apparently or technically of her own free will, but where in reality she was forced out by the actions of her employer.

consultancy 1 The process by which specialist advice, opinion or other service is given to an ORGANIZATION by individuals or GROUPS outside its own STAFF. 2 Individuals or groups offering specialist services, advice or opinions on a professional basis.

consultative committee A COMMITTEE in which representatives of employees in an ORGANIZATION meet regularly with the SENIOR MANAGEMENT, usually to discuss the welfare of the STAFF and the impact on them of policy decisions.

consumer goods Goods for direct consumption, like food, clothing and cars, as opposed to things like machinery and tools which are used to make other goods. Traditionally a distinction has been made between 'consumer disposables' (like food) and 'consumer durables' (like cars), but this distinction is somewhat blurred by the effects of BUILT-IN OBSOLESCENCE.

consumer panel A MARKET RESEARCH technique which uses a representative group of consumers to provide continuous data about specific goods or services. Respondents are usually asked to keep a weekly diary in which they record all relevant purchases. The views of the respondents about these goods and services and their response to ideas for new products are then discussed with them at regular intervals. This technique differs from SURVEY RESEARCH in being a continuous rather than a one-off source of data.

consumerism A movement that looks after the interests of the consumer in the market-place by trying to have the safety, QUALITY and informational content of CONSUMER GOODS and services improved. It can be traced back to the efforts of RALPH NADER in the early 1960s to publicize serious safety hazards in the manufacture of American cars.

contingency planning The attempt to anticipate emergencies or unexpected difficulties that might arise in the future.

contingency theory of leadership Any theory of LEADERSHIP which emphasizes the need for flexibility in dealing with any given situation. The complexity of the modern ORGANIZATION means that effective leadership is contingent upon a great many factors: what may be successful in one context may not be successful in another.

continuous process production A manufacturing technique in which raw materials are fed in at one end of a process and finished products emerge at the other in one continuous uninterrupted flow – hence the alternative name FLOW PRODUCTION. See also for comparison BATCH PRODUCTION and MASS PRODUCTION.

control 1 In terms of ACCOUNTING, control refers to the process of checking actual financial PERFORMANCE against planned performance. 2 In general, the POWER to direct an ORGANIZATION.

controller The SENIOR MANAGER responsible for the finances of an ORGANIZATION.

convergent thinking Thinking along conventional lines in an attempt to find the best *single* answer to a problem, unlike DIVERGENT THINKING. See also LATERAL THINKING.

co-operative A GROUP of producers or purchasers who set up a trading ORGANIZATION, the PROFIT from which is shared out among the members of the group.

copy In ADVERTISING this refers to the text of an advertisement.

copyright The exclusive right to produce or reproduce particular written, musical or artistic material over a fixed period of time. The copyright belongs originally to the creator of the material, who normally assigns it to a publisher in exchange for a ROYALTY on each item sold.

core time Under FLEXIBLE WORK HOURS core time refers to those periods during which all employees must be present at the workplace. The rest of the working day is made up of FLEXIBLE TIME.

corporate image The impression of itself that an ORGANIZATION presents to the outside world.

corporate plan A document that maps out the future WORK and development of an ORGANIZATION over a period of years in the light of its resources and the ENVIRONMENT in which it operates. The plan is concerned with the long-term objectives of the organization and the strategy used to achieve them.

correlation In STATISTICS this refers to the relationship or dependence between two variables. It is measured by a CORRELATION COEFFICIENT.

correlation coefficient In STATISTICS this is a measure (denoted by the letter r) of the extent to which two variables are correlated. It can range from zero CORRELATION to perfect positive correlation (1.00), where the variables are always associated in the same way, or perfect negative correlation (–1.00), where the variables are always associated but in different ways.

Cost-Benefit Analysis A technique for comparing all the costs (both tangible and intangible) of a particular course of action with resulting benefits expected. It normally therefore includes social or environmental costs as well as financial ones.

cost centre A unit whose direct costs can be ascertained and to which fixed costs can be allocated in the pursuit of effective financial CONTROL. This unit may be a department, a place, a person, or even a machine. Contrast with PROFIT CENTRE.

cost effectiveness A measure of the extent to which money has been effectively spent on something. It is found by seeing whether the benefits that have resulted could have been obtained with a lower expenditure. See also VALUE FOR MONEY.

counselling The act of listening to people with personal problems and giving them practical advice. It may happen informally at any level of an ORGANIZATION and, for example, is often done by a FOREMAN for his or her workers. In a more formal sense it is usually seen as a PERSONNEL function where systematic counselling may be given by people, either on a STAFF or CONSULTANCY basis, with appropriate TRAINING in PSYCHOLOGY. This training would probably be based on one of the major theories of psychology like BEHAVIOURISM or PSYCHOANALYSIS or on the NON- DIRECTIVE THERAPY of HUMANISTIC PSYCHOLOGY.

Coverdale training A form of SENSITIVITY TRAINING based on GROUP DYNAMICS developed in the UK by Ralph Coverdale. It emphasizes the performance of real GROUP tasks – as opposed to ROLE PLAYING and is used in MANAGEMENT DEVELOPMENT to improve SOCIAL SKILLS and sharpen COGNITION. See also ACTION LEARNING.

CPA See CRITICAL PATH ANALYSIS.

CPB See COMPUTER-BASED PRACTICE.

creative accounting A form of ACCOUNTING in which the presentation of financial data is manipulated to the advantage of an ORGANIZATION in any way possible within the law (or not, as the case may be).

creative conflict A form of CONFLICT RESOLUTION suggested by the American social worker Mary Parker Follett in the early years of the twentieth century. It advocates that opposing views should not be fudged or compromised or avoided but that a bold attempt be made to examine them with a view to integrating them and moving forward in a way that is in everyone's interest.

creativity The ABILITY to produce new ideas, for example by using DIVERGENT THINKING or INSIGHT.

credit squeeze The governmental control of credit, aimed at making credit more difficult and expensive to obtain, by imposing high interest rates, restrictions on hire purchase and bank lending, and similar measures. The goal is to damp down demand in order to reduce the risk of INFLATION.

crisis management The form of MANAGEMENT adopted in an

emergency or an exceptional situation which focuses all the resources of the ORGANIZATION on getting through a temporary period of difficulty, leaving more fundamental or longer-term issues aside. There is a great temptation for this state of affairs to degenerate into MANAGEMENT BY CRISIS.

Critical Incident Technique   A technique which analyses the impact of key incidents in past PERFORMANCE in order to improve future performance. It is used, for example, to study the safety of equipment in the workplace and in various aspects of MANAGEMENT EDUCATION and TRAINING. It can also be used as the basis for an INTERVIEW during a SELECTION procedure, where inferences may be drawn from a candidate's behaviour during critical incidents in a previous JOB to his likely behaviour in a future JOB.

Critical Path Analysis   A form of OPERATIONAL RESEARCH in which a project is represented by a diagram containing a time schedule for each of the different parts of the project. The 'critical path' through the diagram is then the arrangement of JOBS on the project which will result in the project taking the shortest amount of time, and therefore incurring the least cost. This is a particularly important technique in the planning of large construction projects such as roads and bridges.

cross-sectional research   The study of a relatively large and diverse set of people at a single point in time. Compare with LONGITUDINAL RESEARCH and see also COHORT EFFECT.

culture   In ANTHROPOLOGY a culture is usually defined as the shared beliefs, values, ATTITUDES and expectations about appropriate ways to behave that are held by the members of a social GROUP. This term is also important in PSYCHOLOGY where the *unquestioned assumptions* people share about the world, about the human condition, about what is right, wrong or NORMAL are perhaps even more important.

culture lag   The continued use of outmoded ways of doing things even after the introduction of more effective means for attaining the particular goals of a society, or of an ORGANIZATION. A social version of DECENTRING.

culture shock   The feelings of dislocation and bewilderment that people may experience when they come into contact with a different society or CULTURE. This can even apply to a move from one ORGANIZATION to another where the JOB in question may be similar but the way of doing it very different, e.g. in a move from the PUBLIC SECTOR to the PRIVATE SECTOR, or vice versa.

curriculum vitae From the Latin, meaning 'course of life'. A summary of a person's previous career including work experience, qualifications and achievements and usually some basic BIOGRAPHICAL DATA. It is used by employers in the RECRUITMENT and SELECTION of applicants for jobs.

curve of forgetting A graphic representation of the rate at which the forgetting of learned material occurs. (Fig. 6)

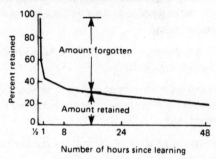

Figure 6 Curve of forgetting

curvilinear relationship A relationship between two variables depicted graphically by a curve rather than a straight line.

customer consciousness Awareness of a customer's needs with regard to a product or service.

customer-contractor principle A term used in the PUBLIC SECTOR to describe research commissioned or sponsored by a government department from a publicly-funded research council. The research council is the contractor, or MIDDLEMAN, for the funds which it awards to professional researchers, and the government department is the end-user or customer for the research findings.

c.v. See CURRICULUM VITAE.

cybernetics From a Greek term meaning something like 'steersman', introduced in 1948 by Norbert Wiener, an American computer engineer. It is usually defined briefly as the study of regulatory mechanisms (like thermostats). Out of this field came the analogy of the brain as a COMPUTER and the MODEL of psychological processes as SYSTEMS of messages with their own built-in FEEDBACK.

D

DAT See DIFFERENTIAL APTITUDE TEST.

data base A store of information, usually held in a COMPUTER, which is logically arranged for a certain use, e.g. a list of people on the payroll.

data processing There are manual, mechanical or ELECTRONIC DATA PROCESSING systems. By any of these means raw information is collected, recorded, organized and analysed, and converted into a form where it may conveniently be used or stored.

David's Dictum In any given ORGANIZATION, at any given time, people are never where they're supposed to be.

day release An arrangement whereby an employee is given time off WORK (usually one day a week), without loss of pay, to further her education or TRAINING with formal study.

de-skilling Any process that reduces the amount of SKILL required for the PERFORMANCE of a JOB.

dead time A term used in PAYMENT-BY-RESULTS schemes. It refers to the time people spend waiting around during WORK hours before they can actually start a piece of work.

decentralization The opposite process to CENTRALIZATION.

decentring The process of continuing to perceive a situation in a way that changing circumstances have rendered ineffective. A psychological version of CULTURE LAG.

decision analysis One of three techniques suggested by PETER DRUCKER to help a WORK ORGANIZATION decide on its most appropriate ORGANIZATIONAL STRUCTURE. This technique is to establish what the key decisions to be made in the organization actually are as opposed to unquestioned assumptions about what they are. The other two techniques are ACTIVITIES ANALYSIS and RELATIONS ANALYSIS.

decision-maker Anyone charged with the formal responsibility for making decisions in an ORGANIZATION. Usually applied to SENIOR MANAGEMENT people.

decision tree A kind of FLOW CHART used to summarize a possible sequence of decisions in which alternative choices are open at each stage and where each alternative is dependent on choices already made.

deduction A sum of money deducted from a given total, e.g. as tax deducted from salary.

deferred compensation Payment made by an ORGANIZATION to its employees at some future date, e.g. as pensions upon RETIREMENT.

deindividuation Feelings of anonymity and being part of a crowd. A blurring of individual IDENTITY and a loosening of INHIBITIONS often follows.

delayed gratification In SOCIOLOGY this term is used for the act of foregoing present satisfaction for the sake of greater satisfaction in the future, e.g. saving money rather than spending it. It is supposed to be most typical of the middle classes in our type of society.

delegation 1 The act of passing AUTHORITY and responsibility for a TASK onto others, usually subordinates in the ORGANIZATION. 2 A GROUP of people with the authority and responsibility for representing a large group.

Delphi method A technique of FORECASTING, using a panel of experts in science and TECHNOLOGY, to predict the likely future of a particular issue. Each member of the panel makes his or her own forecast and the different forecasts are assembled in a composite report which is then sent round the panel for comment. This process is then usually repeated until a workable consensus of the likely future emerges.

demand curve A diagram used to show how much of a certain product is likely to be bought at certain prices. A rise in price for example, usually leads to a fall in demand.

demarcation dispute In INDUSTRIAL RELATIONS this is a disagreement between TRADE UNIONS about the way in which WORK should be divided between different groups of workers, where each union claims the right to do certain types of work exclusively for its own members.

democratic management A type of MANAGEMENT which emphasizes the importance of consulting people about the WORK of the ORGANIZATION and involving STAFF at all levels in the process of making decisions. Usually contrasted with AUTHORITARIAN MANAGEMENT.

demographics A set of figures describing a POPULATION, both in general terms (like births, deaths and marriages) and in specific terms like the consumption of particular goods and services.

denationalization The opposite of NATIONALIZATION. It involves the transfer of state-owned industries or services from the PUBLIC SECTOR to the PRIVATE SECTOR. This is also called PRIVATIZATION.

denial The EGO DEFENCE in which someone simply refuses to accept either that a painful experience has occurred to them or the existence within themselves of an ANXIETY-provoking impulse.

depersonalization The loss of one's IDENTITY or SELF-IMAGE. In a WORK ORGANIZATION this occurs when people are treated like machines. It is often associated with the ASSEMBLY LINE but is more a matter of MANAGEMENT philosophy than PRODUCTION technique as such.

depreciation In ACCOUNTING this is a financial measure of the reduction in value of fixed capital ASSETS over time, e.g. the wear and tear of equipment.

depression 1 In PSYCHOLOGY this is one of the most common forms of emotional disturbance which can vary in intensity from an everyday attack of 'the blues' to a seriously disturbed condition of paralysing hopelessness. It is characterized by ANXIETY, dejection, and a general lowering of activity. There is a difference of opinion as to whether (or to what extent) the causes of depression are to be found in UNCONSCIOUS CONFLICT or in biochemical malfunctioning of the brain. 2 In ECONOMICS, depression also denotes a serious lowering of activity – in business – usually accompanied by high UNEMPLOYMENT and low industrial PRODUCTIVITY.

deprivation The lack of something considered essential to well-being, either psychological, social or material. See also SOCIAL DEPRIVATION.

depth interview An INTERVIEW in which an interviewer tries to get beyond the conscious responses of the interviewee to probe UNCONSCIOUS feelings.

depth psychology The area of PSYCHOLOGY that studies the part the UNCONSCIOUS plays in human behaviour. See also DYNAMIC PSYCHOLOGY.

descriptive statistics STATISTICS that summarize or describe a set of measurements, e.g. MEASURES OF CENTRAL TENDENCY. Compare with INFERENTIAL STATISTICS.

desk research A term used in MARKET RESEARCH to describe the gathering, collation and analysis of available data as opposed to fieldwork which generates fresh data. It is often used as the preliminary stage of a new project. It is the opposite of FIELD RESEARCH.

desktop publishing A feature of the ELECTRONIC OFFICE. A way of preparing documents that involves a MICROCOMPUTER with word processing and COMPUTER GRAPHICS and SOFTWARE which allows a combination of text and pictures to be assembled and displayed on a screen. The final HARD COPY is produced by laser printer.

devaluation The reduction of the offical rate at which the currency of a country is exchanged for other currencies, thereby lowering its value. It has the effect of making imported goods dearer and its own exports cheaper in overseas MARKETS.

deviance Behaviour that is different from the expected NORM of a society.

deviation Generally speaking, a departure from the NORM whether social, psychological or statistical. In STATISTICS it refers to the difference of a given score from the MEAN.

Differential Aptitude Test Actually a battery involving eight different tests of APTITUDES like verbal reasoning and spatial relations. The test is used to assess educational and vocational performance.

differentials In INDUSTRIAL RELATIONS this refers to the differences in levels of PAY between different categories of workers.

differentiation In ORGANIZATION THEORY this term describes the tendency an ORGANIZATION has to set up specialized functions as a way of dealing with increasing complexity in its operations.

diffusion of responsibility In SOCIAL PSYCHOLOGY this is the idea that taking responsibility for initiating action or offering help in an emergency is spread among the people present in the situation. Sometimes the responsibility is so diffuse that no action is taken by anybody. The term can also be used more generally about the diffusion of decision-making responsibility in the presence of other people in a situation.

diminishing returns 1 In ECONOMICS this is the point beyond which any additional input of resources will result in a less than proportionate increase in output. 2 This idea has been borrowed by PSYCHOLOGY where it describes an improvement that gets progressively smaller with each succeeding increment. For example, it is used in the study of LEARNING and MEMORY where, after a large gain at the beginning, extra practice begins to provide less and less gain.

direct labour costs The costs associated with those members of the work-force directly involved in the PRODUCTION of goods and services. Compare with INDIRECT LABOUR COSTS.

direct mail advertising A form of BELOW THE LINE ADVERTISING where COMMUNICATIONS are sent directly to customers or potential customers by mail.

direct taxation The TAXATION of individuals or ORGANIZATIONS on their INCOME or PROFITS, e.g. income tax or capital gains tax. Tax due is paid directly to the government, unlike INDIRECT TAXATION.

directed interview See STRUCTURED INTERVIEW.

discipline In PERSONNEL MANAGEMENT terms this refers to the CONTROL necessary to do a particular JOB, whether externally-imposed or self-imposed, and therefore the basic requirement of all members of a functioning WORK GROUP.

discrimination In PSYCHOLOGY, this is simply the ABILITY to perceive differences. In a social or political context 'difference' often comes to signify something to be feared or rejected, i.e. to discriminate *against*, like sex or colour. This kind of discrimination is usually illegal.

diseconomies of scale The disadvantages resulting from a large, as opposed to a small, scale of operation in an ORGANIZATION. They include difficulties of co-ordination, COMMUNICATION and adaptability to changing circumstances. Compare with ECONOMIES OF SCALE.

dispersion In STATISTICS this term describes the concentration or the spread of scores in a FREQUENCY DISTRIBUTION. The most commonly used measure of dispersion is the STANDARD DEVIATION.

displacement In PSYCHOANALYSIS this is an EGO DEFENCE which involves the UNCONSCIOUS shifting of feeling from its real object to another where it is less threatening to the EGO, e.g. shouting at the television set rather than arguing with the boss.

distance learning A form of LEARNING where learners and teachers are not in face-to-face contact in the same location but communicate at a distance using various techniques. These techniques include AUDIO-VISUAL AIDS; radio, television and video. They also include COMMUNICATION by mail, the original distance learning technique used for many years in correspondence courses.

distributed practice A technique of LEARNING in which the lessons or periods of PRACTICE are spread out as widely as the available time permits. This is a much more effective method of learning in most cases than MASSED PRACTICE, with which it is usually contrasted.

distribution 1 In STATISTICS this is the term for the arrangement of data in categories and their display in the form of a graph or table. 2 In ECONOMICS it is the study of how wealth is spread through a POPULATION.

distributive justice A situation in which everyone receives their just REWARD. Even though this situation does not always occur in real life it has been suggested in PSYCHOLOGY that people need to operate on the basis that it does, i.e. on the basis of a JUST-WORLD HYPOTHESIS.

divergent thinking Creative and original thinking that deviates from the obvious and the conventional to produce several possible solutions to a particular problem. Usually contrasted with CONVERGENT THINKING. See also LATERAL THINKING.

diversification The extension of an ORGANIZATION's activities or products beyond its existing basic range into new areas.

division of labour In ECONOMICS this is a concept introduced by ADAM SMITH in the eighteenth century. It involves breaking down the WORK of an ORGANIZATION into a series of TASKS or operations which allows SPECIALIZATION by workers in one area of activity. See also ASSEMBLY LINE and BUREAUCRACY.

dominance The term used of a strong need to CONTROL, or to be more important than, other people.

double-entry bookkeeping The normal method of BOOKKEEPING or ACCOUNTING in an ORGANIZATION where total credits equal total debits because every transaction is recorded twice, as a credit to one account and a debit to another.

double time A form of OVERTIME working in which time worked is paid at twice the normal rate.

down-sizing A euphemism for REDUNDANCY.

downtime A period of time during which no WORK can be done for reasons beyond the CONTROL of the work-force, e.g. machine failure or bad weather.

downward communication COMMUNICATION from SENIOR MANAGE-MENT to lower levels of employees within an ORGANIZATION.

drive   A general term for a strong urge in an animal or a person, including those urges that are sometimes referred to as instinctive. See also MOTIVATION.

drive reduction   The weakening of a DRIVE in an animal or human, usually as a result of the appropriate needs being satisfied.

Drucker, Peter (born 1909)   An American expert on MANAGEMENT who popularized the concept of MANAGEMENT BY OBJECTIVES and introduced the techniques of ACTIVITIES ANALYSIS, DECISION ANALYSIS and RELATIONS ANALYSIS to the study of ORGANIZATIONAL BEHAVIOUR.

duopoly   A MARKET in which only two firms compete or which is dominated by two firms. See also MONOPOLY and OLIGOPOLY.

dyad   In SOCIOLOGY this is a way of referring to a GROUP of two people.

dynamic psychology   The term applied to those aspects of PSYCHOLOGY that are concerned with MOTIVATION and with understanding causes of behaviour in all its ramifications. PSYCHOANALYSIS and psychoanalytically influenced areas of psychology are the prime, but not the only, examples of dynamic psychology. GESTALT psychology would also qualify, for instance.

dysfunctional   Anything that disturbs the normal FUNCTIONAL operations of an ORGANIZATION. It is used more widely to mean a way of doing things that doesn't work.

E

early retirement   The procedure whereby an employee opts for RETIREMENT before the usual retiral age, usually with an enhanced pension.

econometrics   The branch of ECONOMICS that deals with the mathematical or statistical relationships between economic variables.

economic determinism   The concept that one's place in the economy, or even what one does for a living, determines one's views of society and politics. This concept is usually traced back to KARL MARX.

economic man   An invention of economists to support the belief that the

MOTIVATION of workers depends solely on rational, financial, REWARD and punishment. The beauty of the invention is that it saves them thinking about complicated things like GROUP NORMS or UNCONSCIOUS MOTIVATION.

economics A SOCIAL SCIENCE that deals with the PRODUCTION, DISTRIBUTION and consumption of wealth; of goods and services, and the human activities involved in these processes. It is therefore concerned with issues like business confidence, economic growth, INFLATION and UNEMPLOYMENT.

economies of scale The advantages resulting from a large, as opposed to a small, scale of operation in an ORGANIZATION. They include lower unit costs, greater purchasing power by buying in bulk, opportunities for TRAINING, etc.

EDP See ELECTRONIC DATA PROCESSING

efficacy A term sometimes used in PSYCHOLOGY to describe how effective a person feels in influencing matters of importance to him or her.

ego Latin for the 'I', the conscious awareness of oneself (of one's SELF). According to FREUD the ego is that part of the PERSONALITY closest to external reality which holds the ring between the UNCONSCIOUS drives of the pleasure seeking ID on the one hand and the internalized restrictions of the SUPEREGO on the other. Neurosis, in Freud's view, is thus the result of the ego being unable to maintain harmonious relations with the id and superego because the POWER of their unconscious DRIVES is too much for it to cope with.

ego defence In PSYCHOANALYSIS this is a term for the ways in which the EGO protects itself from the threatening UNCONSCIOUS ideas of the ID or the SUPEREGO, or from external dangers in the ENVIRONMENT. See also, DENIAL, PROJECTION, RATIONALIZATION, REGRESSION, REPRESSION and SUBLIMATION.

Electronic Data Processing Any kind of collection, manipulation or analysis of data that makes use of a COMPUTER.

electronic mail The SYSTEM of transmitting COMMUNICATIONS electronically between individual COMPUTER TERMINALS or within networks of such terminals. It includes the FACSIMILE TRANSMISSION of HARD COPY.

electronic office A term used to describe an (ideal) office which has taken maximum advantage of COMPUTERIZATION and the latest developments in office AUTOMATION and INFORMATION TECHNOLOGY. Such an office would exhibit the following features among others; DESKTOP PUBLISHING, ELECTRONIC MAIL, FACSIMILE TRANSMISSION, MICROCOMPUTERS, TELECONFERENCING, TELEWORKING and WORD PROCESSORS.

email See ELECTRONIC MAIL

empathy The ability to *understand* someone else's feelings, though without actually feeling what she feels. It is regarded in PSYCHOLOGY as an intellectual rather than an emotional experience. Compare with SYMPATHY.

empire-building Seeking the aggrandizement of oneself or of one's ROLE in an ORGANIZATION by the pusuit of greater CONTROL or POWER without regard to the needs of other people or of the organization as a whole.

employee ownership A situation in which the people who work for an ORGANIZATION own some, or even all, of its shares. Figures vary from country to country but most employees own no shares in the organization for which they work. See also EMPLOYEE SHARE OWNERSHIP PLAN.

employee profile Following a JOB ANALYSIS, this is a descriptive list of the background, experience and ABILITY considered necessary for the PERFORMANCE of the JOB.

employee share ownership plan A loan scheme to help employees buy some or all of the shares in their company.

employers' association An ORGANIZATION of employers within an industry or an economy. It is the organization which engages with TRADE UNIONS by representing its members in COLLECTIVE BARGAINING and matters of EMPLOYMENT, as well as lobbying on behalf of its members' interests.

employment Working for someone else in a JOB, usually paid, and part of an ORGANIZATION. See also SELF-EMPLOYMENT and UNEMPLOYMENT.

empowerment Being given the power to do something. This is a term used especially of TRANSFORMATIONAL LEADERSHIP. It denotes the kind of DELEGATION in which the subordinate 'owns' the TASK she has been entrusted with and accepts full responsibility for it, being inspired to extend herself by the force of the vision and commitment she is shown rather than any kind of COERCION.

encounter group A form of PSYCHOTHERAPY conducted in a GROUP rather than with an individual. It has been adapted for use in MANAGEMENT TRAINING generally where people are encouraged to express their emotions and to hear how other people perceive them. The technique may also be used more specifically in ASSERTIVENESS TRAINING.

engineering psychology An American term for ERGONOMICS.

enterprise 1 The willingness to try new initiatives and to accept responsibility and risks. 2 A synonym for a business.

enterprise culture A social climate that celebrates ENTERPRISE and the ENTREPRENEUR.

entrepreneur A person who risks his or her judgement – and often CAPITAL – in a search for PROFIT from new business opportunities. Such a person is considered to have a high NEED FOR ACHIEVEMENT.

entropy In INFORMATION THEORY this is technically an indication of the lack of ORGANIZATION in a SYSTEM, or the degree of openness in the message being conveyed. For example, if a message begins 'the cat...' there is a vast number of possible ways in which the message can be completed, and entropy is therefore high. But if the message reads 'the cat sat on the mat in front of a warm...' it is already highly organized or structured and there is very little choice about the next word. Entropy is therefore low.

environment All the external surroundings of an individual or an ORGANIZATION that affect them in some way.

equity 1 Receiving the same pay as other people doing the same JOB. 2 The ordinary shares in a company.

ergonomics The study of the interaction between people and the ENVIRONMENT in which they WORK, and in particular their relationship to machines and equipment. It draws most heavily on PSYCHOLOGY as well as on anatomy and physiology. The field owes a great deal to the early twentieth century pioneers like FRANK GILBRETH and F W TAYLOR.

ESOP See EMPLOYEE SHARE OWNERSHIP PLAN.

Etzioni model A contribution to ORGANIZATIONAL THEORY by the American sociologist Amitai Etzioni who classified organizations in terms of the kind of POWER or AUTHORITY they used. The typology includes *coercive* (e.g. prisons), *utilitarian* (e.g. business), *normative* (e.g. colleges) and a *mixed* category.

evaluation research The systematic study of the effects and effectiveness of a research or TRAINING or intervention programme.

ex gratia **payment** Payment made as a gift or favour and not in fulfilment of a contract or legal obligation.

exchange rate The rate at which one country's currency can be exchanged for another's.

executive 1 An individual with the AUTHORITY to take decisions in an ORGANIZATION. 2 The people responsible for implementing the decisions of a legislature.

executive search The process of looking systematically for talented EXECUTIVES and offering them an INCENTIVE to move to another ORGANIZATION. See also HEAD-HUNTING.

executive washroom An American term for the lavatory used exclusively by SENIOR MANAGEMENT. The term is used metaphorically to distinguish the people with high status in an ORGANIZATION from the rest. Having the key to the executive washroom is a STATUS SYMBOL.

exercise 1 The use of an attribute like AUTHORITY or POWER. 2 An activity used in TRAINING to analyse or develop a particular SKILL.

exit interview An INTERVIEW with an employee who is leaving an ORGANIZATION to find out the person's reason for leaving and his or her perception of the ORGANIZATION.

expectancy theory of motivation A way of looking at the relationship between MOTIVATION and the PERFORMANCE of a JOB. It suggests that people behave in accordance with the expected outcome of their performance and the value they place on that outcome. Thus people would only be motivated to produce more if they expected that their increased performance would lead to greater satisfaction for them.

expert systems The COMPUTERIZATION of human knowledge, experience and SKILL in a particular field, e.g. banking or medicine. This is a central concern of work in ARTIFICIAL INTELLIGENCE.

extraversion According to the Swiss psychoanalyst Carl Gustav Jung this is a basic PERSONALITY dimension of openness and outward-looking sociability. It is usually contrasted with INTROVERSION.

extrinsic motivation Doing something for reasons of REWARD or punishment external to the activity itself, e.g. staying in a boring JOB because you need the money to pay the mortgage. Usually contrasted with INTRINSIC MOTIVATION.

extroversion More properly EXTRAVERSION.

eye-hand span In ERGONOMICS this is a measure of how far the eye is ahead of the hands in the PERFORMANCE of some manual TASK. It is tested experimentally by suddenly darkening the room and recording how much of the task the subject continues to perform. It is used, for example, in designing keyboards and equipment for sorting letters in the post office.

eye-voice span In ERGONOMICS this is a measure of how far the eye is ahead of the voice in reading out loud. This is tested experimentally by suddenly darkening the room and recording how many words the subject continues to say. It is used in measuring reading SKILLS and in the ASSESSMENT of reading problems.

F

face-to-face group A term used in SOCIAL PSYCHOLOGY, particularly in GROUP DYNAMICS. It describes a small GROUP of people in close enough physical proximity for each person in the group to interact directly with each of the others. Such a group can usually hold no more than six to eight people.

face validity The extent to which a psychological TEST or other procedure appears relevant to the variable it is dealing with. It is also used more loosely in PSYCHOLOGY in the sense of 'having credibility'.

facework In SOCIAL PSYCHOLOGY this term is sometimes used to describe social rituals that save 'face' or enhance a public image at the expense of honest emotion.

facsimile transmission The process of transferring material electronically from one location to another by use of a TELECOMMUNICATIONS network. The image is converted into electronic data which when received is converted back into the original image on paper. Any form of document may be sent or received in this fashion.

factor analysis A technique used in STATISTICS for analysing complex

CORRELATIONS of scores and tracing the factors underlying these correlations.

fatigue   In ERGONOMICS this is a term that includes both the subjective feeling of tiredness that a worker may report and the objectively observed decrease in his or her level of PERFORMANCE of a TASK. The issue of finding the most efficient and effective SYSTEM of WORK and rest periods is of particular importance in matters of safety, e.g. with airline pilots or junior hospital doctors.

FAX   See FACSIMILE TRANSMISSION.

Fayol, Henri (1841–1925)   A late nineteenth century French pioneer of ORGANIZATIONAL THEORY and MANAGEMENT who set out the structural principles of FORMAL ORGANIZATION. The CHIEF EXECUTIVE of a mining company himself, he was mainly interested in SENIOR MANAGEMENT. He believed that general principles of management could be found that were relevant to all kinds of ORGANIZATION and which could be used in MANAGEMENT TRAINING. Fayol is responsible for introducing the concepts, among others, of CHAIN OF COMMAND, JOB DESCRIPTION, MANAGEMENT AUDIT, ORGANIZATION CHART, and SPAN OF CONTROL.

fear of failure   A fear that is aroused when someone feels pressured to achieve something. It is particularly prevalent in people with a high NEED FOR ACHIEVEMENT.

fear of success   Mainly used to describe a motive in some women to avoid doing well and achieving success (especially in competition with men) because their SOCIALIZATION has led them to perceive such behaviour as unfeminine.

featherbedding   1 A restrictive labour practice where more STAFF are employed than is necessary for the WORK to be done. 2 An economic ENVIRONMENT which provides companies with easy profits, e.g. because of the way tax is regulated. 3 The subsidizing of an unprofitable industry by government.

feedback   A term borrowed from CYBERNETICS where it refers to the direct relationship of the input of a SYSTEM to its output. The concept of a return flow of output information which can be used to regulate future input is now widely used in PROGRAMMED LEARNING and the development of TEACHING MACHINES.

Festinger, Leon (1919–1989)   A leading American contributor to

SOCIAL PSYCHOLOGY, best known for his theory of COGNITIVE DISSONANCE.

field research An important part of MARKET RESEARCH. It involves the collection of data about products or ADVERTISING from actual or potential customers, usually by means of INTERVIEW or QUESTIONNAIRE. The opposite of DESK RESEARCH.

field theory In its best known form the GESTALT school of PSYCHOLOGY argued that, in the functioning of the brain and in the behaviour of man and the higher animals, the whole is greater than the sum of all its parts; that the brain could be understood better as a total field than as a collection of nerve cells, and that the cause of a particular piece of behaviour lies in the totality of a field of interacting elements rather than in the most obvious stimulus. In its social applications field theory is closely associated with the work of KURT LEWIN.

FIFO See FIRST IN, FIRST OUT.

fifth generation computer The next generation of COMPUTER, which is currently being planned, and will make use of STATE-OF-THE-ART TECHNOLOGY in design and applications. In particular it is expected to have a more sophisticated MAN-MACHINE INTERFACE – thus making computers more USER FRIENDLY – and new SOFTWARE incorporating principles of ARTIFICIAL INTELLIGENCE intended to help computers approximate more closely in their operations to human COGNITION.

filtering The process of screening out certain stimuli from the ENVIRONMENT, e.g. dust or heat or glaring light. The term is used in PSYCHOLOGY as a metaphor for the way we filter out those sensory stimuli not needed for us to make perceptual sense out of our environment.

financial year The twelve months chosen by an ORGANIZATION as its ACCOUNTING PERIOD.

first in, first out 1 A method of valuing stock or taking INVENTORY in which the prices of the oldest items purchased are applied to the entire stock. Items received first are then first to be sold. 2 A method of choosing people for REDUNDANCY in an ORGANIZATION where the first to be hired are the first to be made redundant.

first-line supervisor The supervisor responsible for the MANAGEMENT of PRODUCTION workers on the SHOP FLOOR. The term refers to anyone at the level above CHARGEHAND and is most often synonymous with the term FOREMAN.

flat organization An ORGANIZATION with relatively few levels in its HIERARCHY. An oft-quoted example is the Catholic Church, with five. Compare with TALL ORGANIZATION.

flexible time Under FLEXIBLE WORKING HOURS flexible time refers to those periods during which an employee may choose whether to be at WORK or not, in contrast to CORE TIME where attendance is mandatory.

flexible working hours A method of organizing working hours which has no fixed starting or finishing times and which allows people some latitude in deciding when they will WORK, provided their daily, weekly or monthly total of hours worked is that contracted for. The working day is divided into CORE TIME and FLEXIBLE TIME. Extra hours worked within a given period may be credited to the next period or given as time off.

flexitime Popular term for FLEXIBLE WORKING HOURS.

float 1 To launch a new company. 2 A small amount of cash used for expenses or in making change. 3 To allow a currency to find its own EXCHANGE RATE in the MARKET, as opposed to maintaining a particular rate by CENTRAL BANK intervention. 4 Used in NETWORK ANALYSIS to denote the amount of time that can be added to a given activity without extending the total time of the whole project.

floppy disk A small magnetic disk inserted into a COMPUTER or WORD PROCESSOR and used for the storage of data. It is called 'floppy' to distinguish it from a hard disk which is a permanent fixture of much higher storage capacity.

flow chart A diagram showing all the parts of a SYSTEM or the stages in a process, and the interrelationships between them, e.g. a map of the London Underground or a plan of a self-assembly wardrobe.

flow production See CONTINOUS PROCESS PRODUCTION.

Ford, Henry (1863–1947) The founder of the Ford Motor Company, best known for inventing the ASSEMBLY LINE form of manufacturing in 1913.

forecasting A series of techniques for trying to predict the future based on known data, usually in regard to the economy or some aspect of it like sales, demand, or the need for MANPOWER PLANNING. Sometimes a QUALITATIVE METHOD like the DELPHI METHOD may be used, but more often a QUANTITATIVE METHOD is used employing a mathematical or statistical technique like REGRESSION analysis. See also MODEL and OPERATIONAL RESEARCH.

foreman A FIRST-LINE SUPERVISOR responsible for a GROUP of workers on the SHOP FLOOR. Usually one level above CHARGEHAND.

form letter A standard letter used for repetitive kinds of correspondence, e.g. rejection slips from publishers.

formal communication COMMUNICATION between people through the official channels of an ORGANIZATION, following the official procedure. Usually contrasted with INFORMAL COMMUNICATION.

formal group A GROUP set up by the MANAGEMENT of an ORGANIZATION with a written mandate and a well-defined purpose. Usually compared with an INFORMAL GROUP.

formal organization The outward face of an ORGANIZATION, as exhibited in its brochure, annual report, rule book, ORGANIZATION CHART and so forth. It represents the official structure of the ORGANIZATION and the way it is supposed to function. Compare with INFORMAL ORGANIZATION.

FORTRAN (Formula Translation) A SYSTEM of words and symbols used in science and TECHNOLOGY to instruct a COMPUTER in its TASK of INFORMATION PROCESSING. See COMPUTER LANGUAGE

free enterprise system An ideal of CAPITALISM in which supply and demand are the only influences on the MARKET and government intervention is minimal, or even less.

free market The kind of MARKET that would exist under a FREE ENTERPRISE SYSTEM.

frequency distribution In STATISTICS this is a tabulation of the number of times something occurs in a body of data.

Freud, Sigmund (1856–1939) A turn-of-the-century Viennese doctor and psychologist. Freud's work may be divided into three areas: his invention of PSYCHOANALYSIS as a therapeutic technique, his theory of PERSONALITY (EGO, ID and SUPEREGO), and his social philosophy. While each of Freud's ideas is still hotly debated, few people would dispute his enormous and widespread influence in making the twentieth century more aware than any previous age of the power of the irrational and the UNCONSCIOUS in human affairs.

fringe benefit A REWARD beyond the basic PAY for the JOB. Examples can range from subsidized meals and travel to pensions, holidays and sickness benefits.

functional Referring to a specialized aspect or function of an ORGANIZATION, like PERSONNEL or MARKETING. Often used more broadly in the sense of something in the organization that is working efficiently.

functional authority The AUTHORITY that is associated with a particular JOB.

functional organization A form of ORGANIZATIONAL STRUCTURE in which specialists carry out their own particular function in an ORGANIZ-ATION (like RESEARCH AND DEVELOPMENT or QUALITY CONTROL) but without any AUTHORITY over people in LINE MANAGEMENT.

functionalism A school of PSYCHOLOGY which emphasizes the functions or activities of the mind rather than its content – which is the emphasis of its rival, STRUCTURALISM.

future shock A term introduced by the American writer Alvin Toffler in the 1970s to denote the growing difficulty many people have in our society of coping with, and adapting to, an increasingly rapid pace of social change.

G

gain-loss theory of interpersonal attraction An attempt in social psychology to formulate a theory that takes account of changes in people's liking for each other. It suggests that *increases* or *decreases* in the reward-ing behaviour we receive from another person have more effect on us than a constant level of liking or disliking. Thus we like best someone who starts out negatively in our estimation and becomes more positive, and we like least a person who starts out positive and becomes negative.

Gallup poll The first and the best-known QUESTIONNAIRE technique for the mass SAMPLING of public opinion. It was invented by the American social scientist George Gallup.

game theory A mathematical approach to the study of CONFLICT and decision-making which treats CONFLICT situations as though they were games, with set tactics and strategies and totally rational players. Some of the simpler situations studied, like the PRISONER'S DILEMMA, have been of interest to people in SOCIAL PSYCHOLOGY looking for a MODEL that would generate ideas about social behaviour.

Gantt chart   A type of BAR CHART developed by HENRY GANTT which is widely used in the PLANNING and CONTROL of PRODUCTION. The chart depicts the progress of a project over time in terms of scheduled PERFORMANCE as compared to actual performance. (Fig. 7)

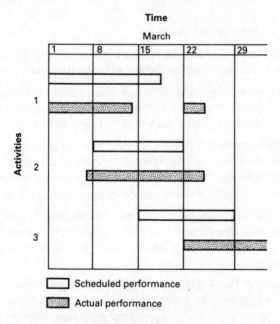

Figure 7   Gantt chart

Gantt, Henry (1861–1919)   An early twentieth century American engineer, and colleague of F W TAYLOR, who was a pioneer of MANAGEMENT CONSULTANCY. He emphasized the importance of employees as HUMAN RESOURCES in an ORGANIZATION and the need to understand their MOTIVATION. He also urged that more social responsibilty be shown by business to society, and he developed the GANNT CHART.

garbage in, garbage out   A slogan coined by people in the COMPUTER industry, but widely adopted outside it, implying that the QUALITY of the output from a SYSTEM depends upon the quality of the input to it.

gatekeeper   **1** In SOCIOLOGY this term is used for someone with the POWER to decide who will join a select GROUP. **2** In ORGANIZATIONAL THEORY the term is used for someone with the power to decide what information will flow into or out of an ORGANIZATION.

Gaussian curve   The BELL-SHAPED CURVE of a NORMAL DISTRIBUTION, named in honour of the nineteenth century German mathematician K F Gauss.

GDP   See GROSS DOMESTIC PRODUCT.

general manager   The MANAGER responsible for the whole range of ADMINISTRATION in an ORGANIZATION and not just a specific function.

generalized other   According to the American sociologist G H Mead, this is the concept an individual has of how other people expect her to behave in a given situation. Compare this with SIGNIFICANT OTHER.

gentleman's agreement   A verbal contract which is not legally binding and depends for its implementation on the sense of honour of the 'gentlemen' involved. This kind of agreement often works as well as, if not better than, the written kind, for example in the diamond business.

gestalt   A German word meaning a form, a configuration, or a whole, which has properties that are more than just the sum of its parts, e.g. the way the brain organizes dots of light into visual patterns, or musical notes into melodies. See also CLOSURE.

Gilbreth, Frank (1868–1924)   An early twentieth century MANAGEMENT scientist who pioneered TIME-AND-MOTION STUDY and contributed generally to the SCIENTIFIC MANAGEMENT movement. Gilbreth was an engineer and worked with his wife Lillian, a psychologist, on many projects. They invented, amongst other things, the SIMO CHART and the THERBLIG.

GNP   See GROSS NATIONAL PRODUCT.

go-slow   A form of INDUSTRIAL ACTION, short of a STRIKE, where workers do not withdraw their labour but slow down the rate at which the WORK is done instead, usually by meticulously following the rule book. See also WORK-TO- RULE.

goal   Something an individual or ORGANIZATION aims to accomplish.

gofer An office junior, one of whose duties is to 'gofer' things and run errands.

golden handcuffs A financial inducement to an employee to stay, so favourable that he or she would find it difficult to leave the ORGANIZATION.

golden handshake A relatively large sum of money given in the form of SEVERANCE PAY for a departure that is usually ahead of normal RETIREMENT or the end of a contract.

golden hello A relatively large payment made to an individual as an inducement to leave one ORGANIZATION and come to another.

golden parachute 1 An American GOLDEN HANDSHAKE. 2 A relatively large sum paid to the directors of the losing company in a TAKEOVER bid should they be made redundant.

goodwill Any INTANGIBLE ASSET of a business which includes its reputation, the LOYALTY of its employees or customers, its location, etc.

grapevine The informal COMMUNICATION NETWORK of an ORGANIZATION. Often much more efficient than the formal one.

graphology The study of handwriting in an attempt to gain a quick insight into someone's PERSONALITY. Often used (or misused) in business as a kind of 'quick and dirty' PROJECTIVE TECHNIQUE.

graveyard shift In SHIFT WORK practice this is a colloquial term for the night shift.

great-man theory The idea that the course of events is influenced at crucial times by the actions of outstanding men. As a way of understanding history it is a gross over-simplification. Despite this it is still popular in the study of LEADERSHIP and its place in the ORGANIZATION.

greenfield site A location for a new commercial or industrial development on which there is no existing or previous development. Originally these locations were, and sometimes still are, 'green fields' on the outskirts of urban areas. A move to such a site is often accompanied by new forms of INDUSTRIAL RELATIONS practices that attempt to overcome traditional MANAGEMENT–TRADE UNION confrontations.

grievance procedure In INDUSTRIAL RELATIONS this is a series of arrangements for settling grievances that employees have against their employers, either directly or between their MANAGEMENT and TRADE UNION representatives.

gross domestic product In ECONOMICS this is the total value of all business activity (all goods and services produced) within a country's economy over a given period of time.

gross national product In ECONOMICS this is the value of the GROSS DOMESTIC PRODUCT plus the value to a country's residents of all foreign investments.

group A number of individuals who are viewed, or who view themselves, as a collectivity. In SOCIOLOGY a group is often classified as a PRIMARY GROUP or SECONDARY GROUP, depending on its size.

group cohesiveness In SOCIAL PSYCHOLOGY this term refers to the tendency of a GROUP to maintain itself in the face of external threats or pressures, based on the attraction the group has for each of its members which acts as a binding force.

group dynamics In SOCIAL PSYCHOLOGY this term refers to the study of the way people behave in a GROUP, especially a small FACE-TO-FACE GROUP. This field is closely associated with the pioneering work of KURT LEWIN.

group mind A hypothetical entity (see HYPOTHESIS), sometimes given mystical qualities, which has been suggested as the agency for crowds acting in unison. It is a way of saying we don't understand very much about crowd behaviour.

group norm Behaviour expected of all the members of a GROUP. In a WORK GROUP the HAWTHORNE STUDIES discovered that this can mean an individual keeping to the same level of PRODUCTIVITY as the other group members, regardless of MANAGEMENT instructions or INCENTIVES. See also NORM.

group process A term used to describe the interactions within a GROUP and the changes that occur over time in the relationships between its members. See also ENCOUNTER GROUP and T-GROUP.

group selection methods Techniques of SELECTION which aim to assess the ABILITY of individuals to WORK with other people in a GROUP. They usually involve the observation of a group of candidates in a discussion or a problem-solving situation.

group structure The way in which a GROUP is designed and organized. It forms the framework for the GROUP PROCESS and for the PERFORMANCE of the group's TASK. Especially important in this context is the COMMUNICATION NETWORK within the ORGANIZATION.

group therapy   A form of PSYCHOTHERAPY which involves several people at the same time. The assumption here is that people can benefit from the experiences and companionship of other people, as well as experiencing the GROUP PROCESS itself.

group training methods   These are TRAINING techniques which use the properties of a GROUP to help individual members learn. The point of the training may be to have the members learn from each other's expertise in tackling a particular problem together, or the point of the group might be the GROUP PROCESS itself from which the members would be encouraged to learn about themselves and how they are perceived by others, as well as about group behaviour in general. See also COVERDALE TRAINING, ENCOUNTER GROUP, SENSITIVITY TRAINING and T-GROUP.

group working   An attempt to increase JOB SATISFACTION (as well as PRODUCTIVITY), especially among ASSEMBLY-LINE workers, by forming individuals into a coherent WORK GROUP and allowing them more autonomy over, and responsibility for, their WORK than they would have as a series of individuals. This process often involves JOB RESTRUCTURING of individual jobs.

grouping   In STATISTICS this is the process of combining individual scores into categories or putting them in RANK ORDER, e.g. as PERCENTILES.

groupthink   George Orwell's term for the totalitarian imposition of authorized thoughts on all the members of a society. The term has been introduced into SOCIAL PSYCHOLOGY by the American scientist Irving Janis, where it is sometimes used to describe the way that members of a very cohesive GROUP can become so preoccupied with maintaining a group consensus of thought that their critical faculties become dulled – sometimes to the point of making a catastrophic decision. See also CONSENSUAL VALIDATION.

growth   **1** In ECONOMICS this is the expansion of a business ORGANIZATION or the economy in general. The rate of growth in the latter is usually measured by the rate of change in the GROSS DOMESTIC PRODUCT. **2** In PSYCHOLOGY the term refers to an increase in maturity as shown by evidence of intellectual or emotional development.

H

habit A learned response to a given situation which occurs in such a regular fashion that it appears to be virtually automatic. Thus it may at times be mistaken for innate behaviour and considered an instinct.

habituation In PSYCHOLOGY this refers to a decreasing response to a stimulus as it becomes more familiar through repeated presentation. With reference to drug use, habituation is the condition, resulting from repeated use of a drug, where there is a psychological, though not a physical, dependence on the drug but with little or no desire to increase the dose.

hacking The unauthorized breaking-in to the DATA BASE of a COMPUTER.

hall test In MARKET RESEARCH this is the technique of asking people their opinions of the ADVERTISING, packaging and presentation of a product.

halo effect In SOCIAL PSYCHOLOGY this refers to the tendency to generalize in judging a person from just one characteristic (usually positive) to a total impression.

handbook A book of instructions on how to operate some machine or procedure. In a more academic sense it is used of a survey of a particular field that is intended to be authoritative and comprehensive.

hard copy A copy on paper, often in the form of print-out, of data stored electronically in a COMPUTER or WORD PROCESSOR.

hard currency A national currency used in international trade because it has a stable or rising EXCHANGE RATE and is generally accepted as being easily convertible, e.g. American dollars or Swiss francs.

hard sell A colloquial term for the aggressive ADVERTISING, MARKETING, PROMOTION and SELLING of a product.

hardware The physical components of electronic and mechanical equipment that make up a COMPUTER, e.g. the disk drives, keyboard, printer, screen, etc. These components must be in place before any SOFTWARE can be added to the SYSTEM.

Hawthorne effect The finding in INDUSTRIAL PSYCHOLOGY that paying attention to people at work improves their PERFORMANCE. Part of the series of HAWTHORNE STUDIES done at the Hawthorne works of the

Western Electric Company in Illinois between 1927 and 1932. Various attempts were made to improve workers' conditions including changes in lighting, rest breaks, hours of WORK, and methods of payment. Each of these changes resulted in an increase in PRODUCTIVITY – and so did a return to the original conditions of work. The investigators concluded that the changes in the external ENVIRONMENT had not influenced the workers' PERFORMANCE so much as their perception that the MANAGEMENT of the ORGANIZATION was interested in them and their work. This is an example of SOCIAL FACILITATION.

Hawthorne studies A series of investigations carried out at the Hawthorne plant of the Western Electric Company in Illinois between 1927 and 1932, under the direction of ELTON MAYO, which marked a turning point in the history of INDUSTRIAL PSYCHOLOGY. The scale of the research was vast – in one phase over 20,000 employees were interviewed – and it explored various aspects of the way in which the employees regarded their WORK, their colleagues, and their supervisors. Apart from the HAWTHORNE EFFECT one other major finding that attracted great attention was that a WORK GROUP could set its own rate of PRODUCTION regardless of external financial incentives offered by MANAGEMENT to the group or to the individuals in it.

head-hunting The process of looking systematically for talented people and offering them an INCENTIVE to move to another ORGANIZATION. A more general form of EXECUTIVE SEARCH.

health and safety at work An area of WORK subject to a great deal of detailed legislation in most industrialized countries because of the importance of labour to PRODUCTIVITY.

hearing loss The degeneration of an individual's hearing ability. Apart from physical damage or disease it can be caused by prolonged exposure to NOISE. Legislation on HEALTH AND SAFETY AT WORK has reduced the serious risk of hearing loss in HEAVY INDUSTRY – though there are still dangers there and in LIGHT INDUSTRY, and even in daily life. (Fig. 8)

heavy industry The term applied to traditional industries like steelmaking, coalmining and shipbuilding which were the basis of western INDUSTRIALIZATION in the nineteenth century and have always required heavy physical labour. Compare with LIGHT INDUSTRY.

hedonism In PSYCHOLOGY this refers to the idea that all of our behaviour stems from the MOTIVATION to pursue pleasure and avoid pain; in

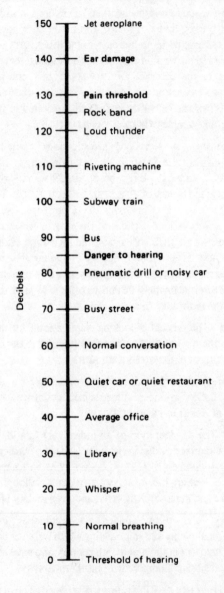

150 —	Jet aeroplane
140 —	**Ear damage**
130 —	**Pain threshold**
	Rock band
120 —	Loud thunder
110 —	Riveting machine
100 —	Subway train
90 —	Bus
	Danger to hearing
80 —	Pneumatic drill or noisy car
70 —	Busy street
60 —	Normal conversation
50 —	Quiet car or quiet restaurant
40 —	Average office
30 —	Library
20 —	Whisper
10 —	Normal breathing
0 —	Threshold of hearing

Decibels

Figure 8   Hearing loss and the loudness of some
familiar sounds

philosophy, the doctrine that it is our ethical duty to do so. The one does not, of course, imply the other.

helicopter factor A term sometimes used in the study of LEADERSHIP to describe the ABILITY to rise above the immediate situation one is in, get a broader perspective on it, and see how it relates to the ORGANIZATION in general.

Herzberg two-factor theory A theory of MOTIVATION proposed in the late 1950s by Fred Herzberg, an American psychologist. Herzberg's theory resulted from a study of JOB SATISFACTION in which he found that satisfaction and dissatisfaction with WORK were caused by different factors. Satisfaction resulted from 'motivators' like recognition and increased responsibility, but dissatisfaction resulted from the working ENVIRONMENT itself and factors like poor physical conditions or relatively low PAY. Herzberg referred to these as 'hygiene factors'. Thus, neither interesting work nor a good working environment were sufficient by themselves – though each was necessary – to ensure job satisfaction. Herzberg's work led to an emphasis on JOB ENRICHMENT schemes.

heuristic An idea or method of teaching that stimulates further thinking and discovery.

hidden agenda Things which are not listed on the formal agenda of a meeting but which influence the meeting nonetheless. There may be unspoken – or even UNCONSCIOUS – ATTITUDES that individuals hold on the subjects under discussion or they may form a quite conscious attempt at manipulating the meeting on behalf of the hidden agenda of an individual or GROUP interest.

hierarchical task analysis A form of TASK ANALYSIS used in assessing TRAINING needs which describes a TASK in terms of a HIERARCHY of the operations necessary for its PERFORMANCE, from the broadest down to the most detailed.

hierarchy 1 Any ORGANIZATIONAL STRUCTURE containing different levels of AUTHORITY, and often responsibility. 2 Any arrangement of things in succeeding levels, each one subsuming all preceding levels.

hierarchy of needs A theory of MOTIVATION proposed by the American psychologist ABRAHAM MASLOW in the 1940s. He suggested there were five distinct levels of human need arranged in a HIERARCHY, starting with the basic physiological needs for food and shelter. As one level of need is satisfied another is reached, until by the fifth level the individual is concerned with the need for SELF-ACTUALIZATION.

histogram In STATISTICS this is a form of BAR CHART on which a FREQUENCY DISTRIBUTION can be represented graphically. (Fig. 9)

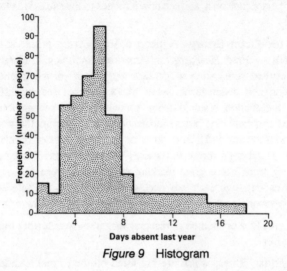

Figure 9 Histogram

home-worker A person who works for an ORGANIZATION at home. This form of working was very common at one time but declined markedly with the twentieth century growth of BUREAUCRACY. But with the development of the ELECTRONIC OFFICE, and a trend towards DECENTRALIZATION, home-working is increasing again. See also NETWORKING.

homeostasis A physiological term for the maintenance of balance or equilibrium within a complex SYSTEM like the human body, or its subsystems like temperature and oxygen level. See also SERVOMECHANISM.

homo economicus The Latin ancestor of ECONOMIC MAN.

horizontal communication COMMUNICATION between people at the same level of the HIERARCHY in an ORGANIZATION. Compare with DOWNWARD COMMUNICATION and UPWARD COMMUNICATION.

horizontal integration The process whereby a company extends its business interests into other geographical areas of the same (or a similar)

MARKET. This is usually accomplished by some form of MERGER with, or TAKEOVER of, another firm in the same business, though sometimes a company is able to extend its PRODUCTION of goods and services by itself. Compare with VERTICAL INTEGRATION.

house journal A magazine or newsletter produced for members of an ORGANIZATION and other interested parties containing news of the organization and its STAFF.

house organ An American HOUSE JOURNAL.

HTA See HIERARCHICAL TASK ANALYSIS.

human asset accounting An attempt to measure the value to an ORGANIZATION of its HUMAN RESOURCES by treating them as ASSETS as well as costs to the organization and assessing, for example, RECRUITMENT and TRAINING policies and funding in this light. Associated with the work of the American psychologist RENSIS LIKERT.

human capital That part of an ORGANIZATION's CAPITAL represented by the ABILITY, experience and SKILL of its work-force.

human communication 1 The process of COMMUNICATION between people. 2 A relatively new field of study involving contributions from COMPUTER science, linguistics, logic, PSYCHOLOGY and SOCIAL SCIENCE.

human engineering An American term for ERGONOMICS.

human factors engineering Another American term for ERGONOMICS.

human performance factors Still another American term for ERGONOMICS.

human relations An approach to ORGANIZATIONAL THEORY that arose in the 1930s in opposition to the SCIENTIFIC MANAGEMENT school. The human relations approach was greatly influenced by the HAWTHORNE STUDIES and the other work of ELTON MAYO, and later by KURT LEWIN and DOUGLAS MCGREGOR. It emphasizes the importance of MORALE in an ORGANIZATION and the need for good working relationships between MANAGEMENT and the people managed, in the quest for organizational effectiveness and high PRODUCTIVITY.

human resource accounting See HUMAN ASSET ACCOUNTING.

human resource management The responsibility for making the best use of an ORGANIZATION's employees. One of the major functions of PERSONNEL MANAGEMENT.

human resource planning See MANPOWER PLANNING.

human resources All the people who WORK for an ORGANIZATION in any capacity.

humanistic psychology A school of PSYCHOLOGY which emphasizes the qualities that differentiate human beings most from other animals, particularly creativity, humour, play and psychological growth in general. It is sometimes known as the 'THIRD FORCE', as opposed to BEHAVIOURISM and PSYCHOANALYSIS. LIKERT, MASLOW and McGREGOR are among its proponents.

hypothesis An explanation put forward to account for observed data, but which has still to be tested.

I

id From the Latin word for 'it'. According to FREUD the id houses the deepest UNCONSCIOUS DRIVES which are most in touch with the biological nature of the body and is one of the three main aspects of the PERSONALITY. The id is dominated by the 'pleasure principle' and causes problems for the EGO when its drives are blocked.

identification In general terms recognizing the IDENTITY or nature of someone or something. In PSYCHOANALYSIS it refers to the phenomenon of emulating the behaviour of a person with whom one has a powerful emotional bond.

identity Having essentially unchanging characteristics. The basic unit of a PERSONALITY, especially the SELF-IMAGE.

identity crisis The acute feeling that one's IDENTITY and sense of SELF have lost their normal stability and continuity over time, leaving one disoriented and having difficulty in recognizing oneself (one's SELF).

ideology In SOCIOLOGY this term refers to a SYSTEM of beliefs that embodies the values of a large GROUP of people. The espousal of the ideology by group members helps to strengthen the GROUP COHESIVE-NESS, e.g. businessmen having the ideology of the FREE ENTERPRISE SYSTEM.

IKBS   See INTELLIGENT KNOWLEDGE-BASED SYSTEM.

illumination   In ERGONOMICS appropriate illumination is a very important aspect of HEALTH AND SAFETY AT WORK.

impersonality   A form of MANAGEMENT that is mechanical in its approach and lacks the personal involvement of a HUMAN RELATIONS emphasis.

implicit personality theory   In PSYCHOLOGY this refers to the unquestioned assumptions an individual uses in thinking about the PERSONALITY of another person. More specifically the term refers to the characteristics that tend to be associated with each other in judging someone's personality. For instance, *'warm'* usually goes with 'outgoing', 'sociable' and 'good-humoured', *'cold'* tends to go with 'withdrawn', 'reserved' and 'humourless'.

impression formation   In SOCIAL PSYCHOLOGY this refers to the process of putting together the various bits of information about someone which we gather in the course of INTERPERSONAL CONTACT, making sense of them in one coherent impression of that person.

impression management   In SOCIOLOGY this is a term introduced by the Canadian sociologist Erving Goffman which describes the attempt to present oneself (one's SELF) to other people in such a way that they will react in a controllable or predictable fashion.

imprest   A cash advance, whether for a FLOAT or to set off against anticipated expenses.

impulse buying   A consumer's purchase of goods without having planned to do so beforehand. The encouragement of impulse buying is the point of displays at supermarket check-out counters.

in-service training   The TRAINING of STAFF by the ORGANIZATION they work for in order to enhance their value to the organization.

incentive   In PSYCHOLOGY this is the basis of MOTIVATION and can refer to any kind of REWARD or inducement. In an ORGANIZATION, especially a business organization, the term is most often applied to financial rewards, although PROMOTION and enhanced STATUS may also be used.

incidental learning   LEARNING that takes place without a conscious effort to do so, e.g. learning the names of shops on the way to the bus stop.

income   This term is usually reserved for money received by an individual, whether *earned* through WORK or *unearned* through dividends, interest, etc.

increment 1 In PERSONNEL MANAGEMENT this is a regular, and usually automatic, increase in a scale of PAY. 2 In ERGONOMICS it may refer to an increase in a stimulus from the ENVIRONMENT of a standard amount, e.g. of ILLUMINATION.

incremental learning LEARNING that takes place in a series of regular and orderly steps rather than following flashes of INSIGHT.

index linking A mechanism for offsetting changes in the value of money by making systematic adjustments to payments, such as pensions, in line with changing prices – usually as reflected in the RETAIL PRICE INDEX.

indirect labour costs The costs associated with those members of the work-force not directly involved in the PRODUCTION of goods and services, but whose labour is essential to the running of the ORGANIZATION, e.g. maintenance and secretarial staff. Compare with DIRECT LABOUR COSTS.

indirect taxation A form of TAXATION which is not paid directly to the government, as in DIRECT TAXATION, but which is added to the cost of goods and services, e.g. value added tax or the television licence in the United Kingdom.

individual differences The comparison of people's characteristics and PERFORMANCE, especially of INTELLIGENCE and INTELLIGENCE TEST scores.

induction The process of introducing new members into an ORGANIZATION. The aim of induction is to provide them with an overview of the whole organization and their place in it, and to give them a taste of the ORGANIZATIONAL CULTURE and the nature of the PSYCHOLOGICAL CONTRACT they will be making

industrial action Any form of collective action taken by the employees of an ORGANIZATION – usually organized by a TRADE UNION – most often to do with PAY or conditions of EMPLOYMENT. Action taken may include a GO-SLOW, STRIKE or WORK-TO-RULE. In some cases employers may take industrial action against their employees by organizing a LOCK-OUT.

industrial democracy A situation in which the MANAGEMENT in an ORGANIZATION or an industry shares POWER with the workers or their representatives in making decisions about their WORK and about the organization in general. See also COLLECTIVE BARGAINING, WORKER-DIRECTORS and WORKS COUNCILS.

industrial disease A disease whose origin is directly attributable to conditions in the ENVIRONMENT of the WORK being done, e.g. the lung diseases of silicosis in miners and asbestosis in building workers.

industrial dispute A CONFLICT between MANAGEMENT and workers or between their representatives, usually about PAY or conditions of EMPLOYMENT.

industrial engineering An American term for a kind of applied ERGONOMICS which concentrates on the SYSTEM of PRODUCTION and draws on various fields, including INDUSTRIAL PSYCHOLOGY, OPERATIONAL RESEARCH and TIME-AND-MOTION STUDY, as well as physics and mathematics.

industrial espionage Spying on an ORGANIZATION to obtain information of economic (or sometimes in an INDUSTRIAL DISPUTE, political) value that the organization wishes to keep to itself. In the United Kingdom stealing a TRADE SECRET is not in itself a criminal offence. Other countries have different laws on industrial espionage.

industrial medicine Medical research and practice carried out in an industrial working ENVIRONMENT and specializing in INDUSTRIAL DISEASE.

industrial psychology The branch of PSYCHOLOGY that deals with the world of WORK, including COUNSELLING, the ENVIRONMENT, HUMAN RELATIONS, JOB ANALYSIS, JOB SATISFACTION, MOTIVATION, RECRUITMENT, SELECTION, TRAINING and, especially, ERGONOMICS. The term is now used interchangeably with OCCUPATIONAL PSYCHOLOGY.

industrial relations This term is now used to describe the web of relationships that exists between employees or their TRADE UNION representatives, MANAGEMENT, and government. Its usage is therefore much broader than its original industrial or manufacturing context and extends to issues and procedures concerning employment in any WORK ENVIRONMENT. See also CLOSED SHOP, COLLECTIVE BARGAINING, INDUSTRIAL ACTION and INDUSTRIAL DEMOCRACY.

Industrial Revolution The Industrial Revolution is the name given to the historical process, beginning in the late eighteenth century, that led to the INDUSTRIALIZATION of the United Kingdom, making it the first industrialized nation and the richest economy the world had ever seen.

industrial sociology The study of the effects of societal processes on the

ENVIRONMENT of WORK and on the economy, e.g. the BLACK ECONOMY, or social change and its effects on economic life.

industrial training In PERSONNEL MANAGEMENT this term usually refers to the TRAINING of new workers in a particular industry or sector of the economy, at all levels of ABILITY and SKILL.

industrial tribunal The SYSTEM of Industrial Tribunals was established in the United Kingdom in 1964, originally to deal with INDUSTRIAL TRAINING disputes, but now deals with a wide variety of disputes between employees and employers such as unfair dismissal or DISCRIMINATION. Each Tribunal consists of three members, including a legally qualified chairman and one nominee from each side of industry. Parties to the dispute may be represented by anyone (e.g. a TRADE UNION official), and not necessarily someone with a legal qualification.

industrialization The term used to describe the process of change in a society from being a largely agricultural economy to an economy dominated by machines, with a concomitant change in the way WORK is organized, featuring a DIVISION OF LABOUR, MASS PRODUCTION and STANDARDIZATION.

inferential statistics Statistical procedures by which generalizations can be made from findings on REPRESENTATIVE SAMPLES to the large GROUPS from which they are drawn.

inferiority complex According to the Viennese psychoanalyst, Alfred Adler, this is an UNCONSCIOUS condition where an individual feels inadequate and resentful, often because of some physical feature regarded as a defect. This complex leads to distorted behaviour, the most striking of which is OVERCOMPENSATION for the perceived defect – a mechanism often invoked to explain aggressiveness in small men.

inflation In ECONOMICS this term describes a situation in which prices are rising relatively quickly, as measured for example by the RETAIL PRICE INDEX, thus causing a fall in the real (as opposed to the nominal) value of money.

inflationary spiral In ECONOMICS this is a situation arising from INFLATION where price rises lead to higher PAY demands which, if satisfied, lead to higher PRODUCTION costs and therefore to still higher prices, and so on.

informal communication COMMUNICATION between people through the GRAPEVINE of an ORGANIZATION. Usually contrasted with FORMAL COMMUNICATION.

informal economy The official name for what is widely known as the BLACK ECONOMY.

informal group Unlike a FORMAL GROUP an INFORMAL GROUP is not set up by the MANAGEMENT of an ORGANIZATION but arises spontaneously in the workplace – where it may not be wholly, or even partly, connected with WORK.

informal organization Unlike the outward face of the FORMAL ORGANIZATION this reflects the inner life of the organization where COMMUNICATION proceeds via the GRAPEVINE, where life is lived in INFORMAL GROUPS and PRODUCTIVITY is determined by the GROUP NORM of a particular WORK GROUP.

information gathering This is the essential first step in setting up an INFORMATION SYSTEM, which requires a procedure for identifying and collecting information.

information management This is concerned with applying INFORMATION TECHNOLOGY to the flow of information in an ORGANIZATION with the intention of ordering it in the best way to achieve ORGANIZATIONAL GOALS.

information overload A situation in which the sheer amount of information in an INFORMATION SYSTEM is simply too great to be coped with by the INFORMATION MANAGEMENT available.

information processing A key term in the study of COGNITION which is used to denote what happens mentally between the stimulus and the response to it, including perception, MEMORY, thinking, decision-making and problem-solving. By 'information' is usually meant any stimulus with a mental content – an image, idea, fact, opinion, etc.

information retrieval The process of recovering data from a DATA BASE. This process lies at the heart of a MANAGEMENT INFORMATION SYSTEM. The most common example of information retrieval is probably the checking by an airline booking clerk of the availability of seats on a particular flight.

information system Any systematic way of organizing the handling of information, from INFORMATION GATHERING to INFORMATION RETRIEVAL and use.

information technology A relatively new field that combines the TECHNOLOGY of the COMPUTER with that of COMMUNICATION. It is concerned with the gathering, recording, storage, processing and dissemination of information and represents the latest form of MAN-MACHINE INTERFACE. See also ARTIFICIAL INTELLIGENCE and SYSTEMS THEORY.

information theory The study of information and the way it is communicated. It originated with mathematicians and engineers and draws heavily on concepts from these fields, but with advances in brain research it has also been used in linguistics and PSYCHOLOGY.

infrastructure The network of essential services supporting a modern society that has undergone the process of INDUSTRIALIZATION, especially education, gas, electricity and transport.

inhibition In PSYCHOLOGY generally this term refers to the blocking of one physiological or psychological process by another, e.g. the response to one sense receptor (the eyes) inhibiting response to another (the ears), or fear inhibiting escape from danger. In PSYCHONALYSIS inhibition is used specifically to describe an impulse from the ID being blocked from entering consciousness by the SUPEREGO. This is not the same as REPRESSION where the impulse is actively held back.

initiating structure The way in which the TASK LEADER of a GROUP organizes it in pursuit of its objectives.

inner-directed A term introduced to SOCIOLOGY in the United States in the 1950s by David Riesman to describe people who interact with their society mainly on the basis of personal values internalized early in life. Contrast with OUTER-DIRECTED and TRADITION-DIRECTED.

innovation The development of something new. It is most often applied to the introduction of new goods and services to the MARKET, particularly those incorporating some advance in TECHNOLOGY.

inoculation In SOCIAL PSYCHOLOGY this is a technique for strengthening someone's ATTITUDE on an issue, and his resistance to persuasion, by exposing him to a small dose of the opposing attitude.

input-output analysis This is a set of STATISTICS used in a general sense in ECONOMICS, and more specifically in MARKETING and MARKET RESEARCH, in which patterns of buying and selling between industries or sectors of an economy are analysed to study changes in their trading relationships over a given period of time. This technique is particularly useful in spotting changing trends in consumer choices.

INSET See IN-SERVICE TRAINING.

insight learning A form of LEARNING in which there appears understanding – usually sudden – in dealing with a problem. Insight learning involves both COGNITION, in finding a solution to a practical problem, and the SELF-KNOWLEDGE that can be achieved in PSYCHOTHERAPY. It is usually compared with TRIAL AND ERROR LEARNING or ROTE LEARNING.

institution In SOCIAL SCIENCE this term refers to a social, cultural, economic or political arrangement that may be of greater or lesser importance to people's lives – like the family or the monarchy – but which usually endures over time and reflects some basic values of the society. When an individual ORGANIZATION has endured long enough it is often accepted as an institution, e.g. the Bank of England or the BBC.

institutional investor An ORGANIZATION that invests in shares and other securities with funds obtained from a large number of individual savers e.g. a bank, insurance company or TRADE UNION.

institutional racism Behaviour exhibiting racial PREJUDICE which has not been adopted by choice but is simply the consequence of CONFORMITY to the NORMS and conventions of a society whose INSTITUTIONS of law, government and business systematically discriminate against particular racial GROUPS.

instrumental aggression A term used in SOCIAL PSYCHOLOGY to describe behaviour that is not aggressive for its own sake but as a means to an end. For example, the difference between killing an enemy in a face-to-face confrontation and pressing a button in a missile site a thousand miles away.

intangible assets ASSETS which have no physical existence (unlike, say, machinery or property) but which are still presumed to be of some financial value to the ORGANIZATION, e.g. COPYRIGHT, GOODWILL, PATENT or TRADE MARK.

integration The process of organizing different parts into a whole of a higher order. It is used widely in science, from the ORGANIZATION of nervous impulses necessary for any kind of behaviour up to the organization of a whole society. In both individual PSYCHOLOGY and

ORGANIZATIONAL PSYCHOLOGY integration is widely regarded as the key criterion of healthy functioning.

integrative bargaining A form of BARGAINING whose objective is to achieve an outcome in which both parties gain.

intelligence Although this concept has been discussed in PSYCHOLOGY since the 1870s there is no universally accepted agreement on what intelligence is. Most psychologists would probably agree that heredity sets the limits of a person's intelligence and most would also agree that the ABILITY to think in one form or another (handling abstract ideas, adapting to new situations, perceiving complex relationships) is a sign of high intelligence – which may not get us very far but has never prevented psychologists from designing new INTELLIGENCE TESTS.

intelligence test A TEST that is supposed to measure INTELLIGENCE, whatever that may be. Its purpose is to discriminate between people who score high and people who score low (ie. high and low IQ), for the purpose of assigning them to various educational, occupational and social categories. High scores are supposed to denote high intelligence, and vice versa, but in the absence of an agreed definition of intelligence the OPERATIONAL DEFINITION becomes circular – people score high on intelligence tests because they are highly intelligent because highly intelligent people score high on intelligence tests. There is also a great deal of evidence that intelligence tests, which are usually highly verbal, tend to be biased in favour of white, urban middle-class people in their SELECTION of test items. See also IQ.

intelligent knowledge-based system The branch of ARTIFICIAL INTELLIGENCE whose objective is to develop COMPUTER SYSTEMS resembling various aspects of human INTELLIGENCE, e.g. language ABILITY and LEARNING capacity.

intercorrelations A table of CORRELATIONS between each and every one of a series of variables.

interference This term has two principal meanings in PSYCHOLOGY: the change in perception when two light or sound waves out of phase come together and, more commonly, where one kind of LEARNING disturbs another or leads to INHIBITION of it.

intergroup relations In SOCIAL PSYCHOLOGY this term refers to the relations *between* one GROUP and any other groups. Compare with INTRAGROUP RELATIONS. See also SUPERORDINATE GOAL.

internal justification In SOCIAL PSYCHOLOGY this is a way of resolving COGNITIVE DISSONANCE and underlies the most powerful kind of ATTITUDE change, e.g. if you feel, on reflection, that you have an awful job, you can resolve (psychologically) the dissonance between the COGNITIONS 'I am a sensible person' and 'I choose to work in an awful job' either externally or internally. An *external* justification might be 'I do it for the money', but that wouldn't change your opinion of the JOB. However, if you began to consider the job in a different light and saw its more positive aspects you would be justifying your decision to stay in an awful job *internally*. You would in fact be persuading yourself, the most powerful way of changing anyone's attitudes.

internalization In PSYCHOLOGY this is the process of accepting external ideas or values as one's own to the point of not being aware of their origins. The best known example of this concept is the SUPEREGO, where the values of the parents and the parent society are internalized into the developing PERSONALITY.

interpersonal attraction The general term for an area of SOCIAL PSYCHOLOGY concerned with why people are attracted to each other. For a specific term see GAIN-LOSS THEORY OF INTERPERSONAL ATTRACTION.

interpersonal conflict The general term for any kind of CONFLICT between individuals (as opposed to GROUPS).

interpersonal contact The general term for any kind of contact, of any type or duration, between individuals (as opposed to GROUPS).

interpersonal relations The general term for any kind of relationships or forms of COMMUNICATION between individuals (as opposed to GROUPS).

interpersonal skills development A GROUP TRAINING METHOD which emphasizes the SKILLS involved in COMMUNICATION with other people in listening to their replies. These skills are obviously important throughout the life of an ORGANIZATION but are perhaps most visible (on both sides of the table) in an INTERVIEW, especially a PERFORMANCE APPRAISAL INTERVIEW.

interview In essence an interview is a form of conversation, between one interviewee and one or more interviewers, which is structured to a greater or lesser extent. It is probably the most widely-used method for the ASSESSMENT of a person's ABILITY. It is also the most subjective method

and one which is extremely difficult for the interviewer to do well. See also
INTERVIEWER BIAS.

interviewer bias The effects on an INTERVIEW of the conscious and
UNCONSCIOUS biases (assumptions, expectations) of the interviewer. See
also SELF-FULFILLING PROPHECY.

intragroup relations In SOCIAL PSYCHOLOGY, this term refers to the
relations between its members *within* the GROUP. Compare with
INTERGROUP RELATIONS. See also SUPERORDINATE GOAL.

intrinsic motivation Doing something for its own sake, because the
activity itself constitutes a REWARD. Always contrasted with EXTRINSIC
MOTIVATION.

introversion According to the Viennese psychoanalyst, Carl Gustav Jung,
this is a basic PERSONALITY dimension of being withdrawn, inward-
looking and passive that is usually contrasted with EXTRAVERSION.

inventory In ACCOUNTING, this term has three related uses: **1** a list of
items in stock; **2** a list of raw materials; **3** the cost of materials currently
being processed.

investment In ECONOMICS this is the general term for spending money,
usually from current INCOME on the ASSETS of an ORGANIZATION
(including its human assets) in order to expand and increase PRODUCTION
in the future.

invisible hand In ECONOMICS this refers to the term invented in the
eighteenth century by ADAM SMITH to support the policy of free trade as
opposed to government intervention in the workings of the MARKET. The
pursuit of self-interested economic behaviour by each individual was
supposed to lead naturally, when aggregated, to the best interests of the
whole society being served – as if by the workings of an 'invisible hand'.
This idea is frequently claimed as the basis of the modern IDEOLOGY of
the FREE MARKET.

IQ The Intelligence Quotient; a score obtained from an INTELLIGENCE
TEST by dividing the mental age (MA) obtained on the test by the actual
or chronological age (CA) and multiplying by 100,

i.e. $$IQ = \frac{MA}{CA} \quad 100$$

An IQ score by itself is meaningless. It does not measure INTELLIGENCE
the way a tape measures height, for instance. It is only a measure of

comparison between all the people who have taken that particular test, with the average score being placed arbitrarily at around 100

IT See INFORMATION TECHNOLOGY.

item analysis In STATISTICS this is a technique to determine the effectiveness of different items on a TEST in its DISCRIMINATION among the people who take it.

iterative process 1 In OPERATIONAL RESEARCH, this refers to a mathematical technique for making successive approximations in the search for a solution by the method of repeated calculations. 2 In a BUREAUCRACY, especially in the PUBLIC SECTOR, the term is used to denote a dialogue or a series of consultations back and forth, in the formulation of a policy document.

J

J-curve 1 In PSYCHOLOGY this term denotes a FREQUENCY DISTRIBUTION of conforming behaviour, portraying on a graph that the behaviour of most people in a given situation will fall at or near the behaviour expected. The curve looks roughly like a capital J, or a reverse J, in shape. 2 In ECONOMICS, the curve depicts a small decrease in some variable followed by a large and rapid increase.

jargon A private language, spoken by a GROUP in the conduct of its affairs, which is usually impenetrable – intentionally – to outsiders, i.e. the 'lay public'. It serves to enhance GROUP COHESIVENESS and the SELF-ESTEEM of its members, e.g. computerese and legalese. See also PROFESSION.

jet lag The physiological effects and psychological STRESS caused by having to adjust one's CIRCADIAN RHYTHM to the disorienting effects of rapid long-distance air travel that passes through different time zones.

JIT See JUST-IN-TIME PRODUCTION.

j.n.d. See JUST NOTICEABLE DIFFERENCE.

job A piece of WORK or an order for a piece of work to be done. The term is also used more widely to describe one's livelihood. A job is therefore a unit of work large enough to be the basis of an occupation.

job analysis A key ROLE for practitioners of INDUSTRIAL PSYCHOLOGY where the elements making up a JOB are studied in an attempt to match the TASKS and SKILLS necessary for successful PERFORMANCE with the ABILITY of the worker to perform them. Job analysis is an essential prerequisite for the study of jobs and job-holders and is therefore an important tool of PERSONNEL MANAGEMENT.

job costing A method for calculating costs in an area where each JOB constitutes a separate order or finite unit of WORK. This is considered particularly appropriate for CONSULTANCY work, e.g. in building or qualitative MARKET RESEARCH.

job demands The requirements a JOB has, and therefore what will be expected of the person who performs it.

job description The broad outline of what TASKS a JOB consists of, delineating its duties and responsibilities and the position of the job within the ORGANIZATION.

job design The process of relating all the TASKS to be performed within an ORGANIZATION to specific JOBS.

job enlargement Expanding the content of a JOB to include new responsibilities, that will usually require TRAINING and the acquisition of new SKILLS.

job enrichment The desired result of JOB RESTRUCTURING, in which various aspects of a JOB or its component TASKS are changed in order to help strengthen employee MOTIVATION and increase JOB SATISFACTION.

job evaluation A method of comparing jobs for their relative value to an ORGANIZATION and then determining on this basis a HIERARCHY of PAY appropriate to each JOB. The method uses such factors as complexity, experience, responsibility, SKILL, etc.

job fragmentation Splitting an existing JOB up and dividing it amongst other jobs, or creating a new series of smaller jobs.

job longevity The concept that length of time spent in a JOB is an important factor in determining what contributes most to an individual's JOB SATISFACTION. For example, there is evidence that, after five years in a job, factors in the organizational ENVIRONMENT like PAY, FRINGE BENEFITS, and relationships with colleagues and supervisors are more important than the PERFORMANCE of the job itself.

job mobility The extent to which workers are prepared to change JOB, especially if a change requires geographical relocation.

job redesign Doing a new JOB DESIGN as part of a wider process, like JOB ENLARGEMENT or JOB ENRICHMENT, and preparatory to JOB RESTRUCTURING.

job restructuring Making changes in the TASKS and responsibilities of an *individual's* JOB rather than any change in ORGANIZATIONAL STRUCTURE or GROUP WORKING practices, though the latter would lead to job restructuring. The addition of similar tasks as a result of job restructuring would mean JOB ENLARGEMENT; an increase of responsibility and different types of task would be JOB ENRICHMENT.

job rotation The systematic moving of people at the same level in an ORGANIZATION from one JOB to another. On the SHOP FLOOR it is done to relieve boredom and monotony; as part of MANAGEMENT DEVELOPMENT it is done to give MANAGERS a broader experience of the ORGANIZATION.

job satisfaction The extent to which a worker is content with the REWARDS she gets out of her JOB, particularly in terms of INTRINSIC MOTIVATION.

job security The right to continued EMPLOYMENT, usually until RETIREMENT. Contractually this is now quite rare; psychologically the feeling of security varies with the JOB and the employee.

job sharing The procedure whereby two (or more) part-time workers make up one full-time JOB between them and share the accompanying PAY on a pro rata basis.

job simplification The process of using people like machines by reducing their JOB to consist of the smallest TASK possible with the least amount of discretion in it. It is particularly associated with WORK on an ASSEMBLY LINE. Compare with WORK SIMPLIFICATION.

job specification A much more detailed version of a JOB DESCRIPTION, stating as exactly as possible what a JOB entails. It is usually drawn up on the basis of a JOB ANALYSIS.

job title The official name an ORGANIZATION gives to the occupant of a particular JOB, e.g. sales MANAGER.

job transition The process of moving from one JOB to another, either within the same ORGANIZATION or between organizations. A time of heightened psychological activity and STRESS.

joint consultation A procedure whereby employees and employers in an ORGANIZATION (or their representatives) have a forum for discussing such common concerns as DISCIPLINE, TRAINING, or the WELFARE FUNCTION.

journeyman The traditional term for a skilled worker who has completed a craft or trade APPRENTICESHIP but is not yet a master craftsman in SELF-EMPLOYMENT. In previous times such a worker would need to travel around offering his SKILLS to a master until such time as he could set up in business for himself.

junior management The term applied to MANAGERS who are relatively low in the HIERARCHY of an ORGANIZATION because they are junior in age and/or level of responsibility and AUTHORITY.

just noticeable difference In ERGONOMICS this is the minimum amount of difference that a subject can detect between two stimuli.

justification The procedure used by a WORD PROCESSOR to line up the right hand margin of a page so that all the lines of script are of equal length.

just-in-time production A Japanese approach to the process of PRODUCTION which emphasizes tight scheduling of materials into and out of the process, with a very low INVENTORY of stock carried on-site. The aim of the process is to prevent bottle-necks in production and ensure a smooth flow of THROUGHPUT. It is also claimed that this approach reduces costs, increases JOB SATISFACTION and improves QUALITY.

just-world hypothesis The term used in SOCIAL PSYCHOLOGY for the unquestioned assumption that the world is a just place, where the deserving receive a proper REWARD and the undeserving are punished. It therefore follows that if people are punished they must have done something to deserve it, and this is how the HYPOTHESIS accounts for people who blame victims for their own misfortunes. See also DISTRIBUTIVE JUSTICE.

K

k A common abbreviation for one thousand, derived from the French 'kilo'. It is used especially of money, e.g. 50K = £50,000.

kaizen The Japanese concept of continuous improvement. The basis for a policy of TOTAL QUALITY, it applies both to HUMAN RESOURCES and the use of machinery.

kanban The basis for the Japanese SYSTEM of JUST-IN-TIME PRODUCTION. It involves requesting items only as they become necessary in the PRODUCTION process.

Kelly repertory grid A technique used in MARKET RESEARCH to obtain opinions from respondents about products and their BRAND images. The materials are presented in threes and the respondents are asked to say why one is different from the other two and why these two are similar.

Keynes, John Maynard (1883–1946) An influential British economist, active in the 1930s, who believed that an economy could not regulate itself in the interests of the society as a whole via the FREE MARKET. He suggested that general prosperity, and full EMPLOYMENT in particular, required government spending and INVESTMENT.

kinaesthetics The study of body movements. It is used in TIME-AND-MOTION STUDY and WORK STUDY.

kinesics The study of body movements in NON-VERBAL COMMUNICATION.

knowledge-based industry A term used of a field that deals in the COMMUNICATION of information, and particularly in INFORMATION MANAGEMENT.

knowledge engineering A term sometimes used of a group of techniques, based on theories of ARTIFICIAL INTELLIGENCE, which is concerned with the design of INTELLIGENT KNOWLEDGE-BASED SYSTEMS.

knowledge of results The process of giving people FEEDBACK on their PERFORMANCE of a TASK. In the study of LEARNING this has been found to increase someone's MOTIVATION to perform better.

knowledge worker A term sometimes used of a person working in the COMMUNICATION of information, particularly in INFORMATION MANAGEMENT.

Kondratieff cycle The term given in ECONOMICS to a phenomenon first noticed by the nineteenth century Russian economist Nikolai Kondratieff. This was the appearance of long, but regularly occurring, cycles or waves in economic activity that oscillated between boom and RECESSION every fifty years or so.

Kuder Preference Record This is a QUESTIONNAIRE technique, used in OCCUPATIONAL PSYCHOLOGY, which is designed to elicit a subject's areas of vocational interest. It is named after its designer, the American psychologist George Kuder.

L

labelling theory In PSYCHOLOGY, this is a way of explaining DEVIANCE by focusing on the reactions of other people to the person they label deviant. When combined with SELF-FULFILLING PROPHECY, labelling theory has also been used to account for very disturbed, or psychotic, behaviour. Thus, if a person is labelled paranoid everything she does is interpreted in the light of her paranoia and invariably then taken as evidence for the correctness of the original diagnosis.

labour-intensive The term used for relying mainly on labour in the PRODUCTION of goods and services, as opposed to the INVESTMENT of CAPITAL in the process of AUTOMATION, e.g. as in teaching or tailoring. It is therefore the opposite of CAPITAL-INTENSIVE.

labour mobility See JOB MOBILITY.

labour relations See INDUSTRIAL RELATIONS.

labour turnover The percentage of the total labour force of an ORGANIZATION leaving its EMPLOYMENT and being replaced over a given period of time, usually a year.

laissez-faire **economy** From the French for 'let do'. This is the term used in ECONOMICS for the traditional doctrine that a government should not intervene in the workings of its country's economy. The basis for the FREE ENTERPRISE SYSTEM.

last in, first out 1 A method of valuing stock or taking INVENTORY in which the prices of the newest items purchased are applied to the entire stock. Items received last are then first to be sold. **2** A method of choosing people for REDUNDANCY in an ORGANIZATION where the last to be hired are the first to be made redundant.

lateral communication   See HORIZONTAL COMMUNICATION.

lateral integration   See HORIZONTAL INTEGRATION.

lateral mobility   Sideways JOB MOBILITY in the same ORGANIZATION at the same level of AUTHORITY and responsibility.

lateral thinking   A term suggested by the British psychologist Edward de Bono to describe an attempt to solve a problem by any means other than the usual straight-line method of thinking, thus allowing the problem to be re-conceptualized and perhaps solved by a previously unacceptable or unthought-of solution.

LCU   A LIFE CHANGE UNIT.

lead time   The time taken to complete a cycle of activity. The term is usually used in reference to the PRODUCTION process, from the initial idea to the finished product, although it can also refer to the time-lag in supplying an order.

leadership   **1** A widely-applied term that usually refers to the PERSONALITY characteristics and the behaviour of people with AUTHORITY and influence and responsibility for leading GROUPS. See also GREAT-MAN THEORY, LEADERSHIP STYLE and RENSIS LIKERT. **2** The term is also used to refer to the GROUP of people officially responsible for running an ORGANIZATION.

leadership style   This term usually refers to the adoption of an AUTHORITARIAN MANAGEMENT or a DEMOCRATIC MANAGEMENT style by an individual in an ORGANIZATION, depending on which style is more comfortable to his or her PERSONALITY.

learning   A term with a very wide application in PSYCHOLOGY, TRAINING and beyond. It is usually taken to be the process of acquiring knowledge or SKILLS.

learning curve   The curve obtained by plotting on a graph measured changes in the PERFORMANCE of LEARNING over time.

learning plateau   A flattening of the LEARNING CURVE due to a temporary halt in LEARNING progress.

learning set   Sometimes described as 'learning how to learn', this is a

Rank	Life event	Value
1	Death of spouse	100
2	Divorce	73
3	Marital separation	65
4	Jail term	63
5	Death of close family member	63
6	Personal injury or illness	53
7	Marriage	50
8	Fired at work	47
9	Marital reconciliation	45
10	Retirement	45
11	Change in health of family member	44
12	Pregnancy	40
13	Sex difficulties	39
14	Gain of new family member	39
15	Business readjustment	39
16	Change in financial state	38
17	Death of close friend	37
18	Change to different line of work	36
19	Change in number of arguments with spouse	35
20	Large mortgage or loan	30
21	Foreclosure of mortgage or loan	30
22	Change in responsibilities at work	29
23	Son or daughter leaving home	29
24	Trouble with in-laws	29
25	Outstanding personal achievement	28
26	Wife begins or stops work	26
27	Begin or end course of study	26
28	Change in living conditions	25
29	Revision of personal habits	24
30	Trouble with boss	23
31	Change in work hours or conditions	20
32	Change in residence	20
33	Change in place of education	20
34	Change in recreation	19
35	Change in church activities	19
36	Change in social activities	18
37	Small mortgage or loan	17
38	Change in sleeping habits	16
39	Change in number of family get-togethers	15
40	Change in eating habits	15
41	Vacation	13
42	Christmas	12
43	Minor violations of the law	11

Figure 10   General stress scale
(adapted from Holmes, T H and Rahe, R H (1967) 'The social
readjustment rating scale', *Journal of Psychosomatic Research* 11:
213–18)

generalized approach to problems in which people carry over into a new LEARNING situation the responses and strategies they learned in a previous situation. TRANSFER OF TRAINING results from a learning set.

learning theory In PSYCHOLOGY this refers to the systematic attempt to explain the process of LEARNING.

least preferred co-worker A technique developed by the American psychologist Fred Fiedler to assess the extent to which someone in a position of LEADERSHIP is predisposed to deal more with the TASK confronting the GROUP or the INTERPERSONAL RELATIONS of its members. The technique involves asking people about their 'least preferred co-worker'. Someone with negative views of this colleague has a low LPC score and, it is assumed, is predominantly a TASK LEADER. Someone with a more positive view would therefore have a high LPC score and be more concerned with maintaining harmony and cordiality within the group (ie. a SOCIAL-EMOTIONAL LEADER) than with the PERFORMANCE of the task.

legitimacy A term sometimes used of the LEADERSHIP of a GROUP or ORGANIZATION when it is fully accepted by the members.

level of aspiration The goals or standards of PERFORMANCE a person sets for herself.

levels of significance See STATISTICAL SIGNIFICANCE.

Lewin, Kurt (1890–1947) A German psychologist who escaped from Nazism and went to the United States in the 1930s. He was a student of the early GESTALT psychologists who applied much of their thinking to SOCIAL PSYCHOLOGY, in which he pioneered the field of GROUP DYNAMICS as well as the HUMAN RELATIONS school of MANAGEMENT. See, for example, his work on LEADERSHIP STYLE.

lie detector An instrument for monitoring physiological changes like heart rate and electrical resistance of the skin under conditions of emotional STRESS. It is sometimes used in sensitive governmental areas of EMPLOYMENT. The assumption is that the subject will show measurable signs of emotional upheaval if he lies in answer to a question – a very big assumption.

Life Change Unit An item in a rating scale of stressful incidents drawn up by a group of American psychologists. The bigger the event, or change, in a person's life the greater the likely STRESS. Top of the scale is the death of a spouse. But stressful events (or LCUs) are not necessarily or entirely painful; marriage is also high on the list. (Fig. 10)

LIFO See LAST IN, FIRST OUT.

life space A term introduced by KURT LEWIN to describe the totality of the physical and psychological factors in the ENVIRONMENT of an individual or GROUP at any given time.

light industry The term applied to industries like electronics or clothing, which tend to be smaller in scale and to require less physical labour than HEAVY INDUSTRY.

Likert, Rensis An American psychologist whose contributions to the study of MANAGEMENT and ORGANIZATIONAL THEORY include the concepts of HUMAN ASSET ACCOUNTING, the LIKERT SCALE, the LINKING-PIN MANAGEMENT STRUCTURE, and SYSTEM 4.

Likert scale A QUESTIONNAIRE scale developed by the American psychologist Rensis Likert which allows respondents to indicate how much they agree or disagree with a series of statements on a three- or five-point scale, as opposed to the more simplistic choice of either/or responses. It is widely used in ATTITUDE studies.

line and staff concept A term used in ORGANIZATIONAL THEORY to denote the different functions performed in an ORGANIZATION by MANAGERS who are directly responsible for achieving the organization's GOALS ('line') and those who perform supportive functions like MARKETING or PERSONNEL ('staff'). This distinction becomes somewhat blurred in practice. See also LINE MANAGEMENT and STAFF MANAGEMENT.

line management The term used to describe MANAGERS who are responsible for an ORGANIZATION carrying out its basic functions, e.g. MARKETING, PRODUCTION, etc., and who give and receive orders via the CHAIN OF COMMAND, within the organizational HIERARCHY. Compare with STAFF MANAGEMENT.

line of command See CHAIN OF COMMAND.

line relationship A LINE MANAGEMENT relationship between a superior and a subordinate in the HIERARCHY of the ORGANIZATION.

linear programme A mathematical technique used in OPERATIONAL RESEARCH to help the DECISION-MAKER where there is a direct, straight-line relationship between two variables, e.g. where the shortest route means the lowest cost.

linear relationship The relationship between two or more JOBS in an ORGANIZATION as plotted on an ORGANIZATION CHART.

linking-pin management structure A way of conceptualizing ORGANIZATIONAL STRUCTURE, developed by the American psychologist RENSIS LIKERT where an ORGANIZATION consists of a series of interlocking GROUPS connected up into a coherent SYSTEM by key individuals each of whom has overlapping group membership. These members are the 'linking pins' in the system.

liquid assets ASSETS that are in cash and immediately available or that are easily convertible into cash, like securities or bank deposits.

lock-out Action taken by employers in the course of an INDUSTRIAL DISPUTE which involves denying the workers access to the workplace by locking them out; i.e. it is the opposite to a STRIKE in its effect.

locus of control A dimension of PERSONALITY in which people who have an *internal* locus feel they have control over what happens to them, and people with an *external* locus tend to attribute their experiences to outside forces or other people.

logistics A term that was originally used in the military sphere to describe the organizing and moving of troops and equipment. It is now often applied to any detailed planning process in an ORGANIZATION which entails the DISTRIBUTION or redistribution of resources.

logo 1 Short for logotype, the trademark or other identifying symbol of an ORGANIZATION, often including the name. (Fig. ll) 2 A high-level COMPUTER LANGUAGE.

Figure 11 Logo

long-range planning What a CORPORATE PLAN is used for.

long-term unemployment A term normally reserved for a period of UNEMPLOYMENT of twelve months or longer.

longitudinal research   Repeated study of the same people over a period of time. Compare with CROSS-SECTIONAL RESEARCH and see also COHORT EFFECT.

longwall method   A method of PRODUCTION in the United Kingdom coal-mining industry which led to a change in SHIFT WORK and other practices as the result of the introduction of new mining TECHNOLOGY. These changes meant there was one long coal-face of two hundred yards being worked by three shifts of miners with different TASKS as opposed to one team on a ten-yard face who did the whole JOB. This resulted in social and PSYCHOSOMATIC DISORDERS which were dealt with by treating the new workplace as a SOCIO-TECHNICAL SYSTEM.

looking-glass self   In SOCIOLOGY this term is used for the part of a person's SELF-IMAGE that is based on the reactions or judgements of other people. The term was suggested by two American sociologists in the 1920s, C H Cooley and G H Mead.

loss leader   In MARKETING this refers to a product or service sold at a loss for the seller in order to attract customers to buy other products or services.

loyalty   Usually defined as the dedication of people to a GROUP and its objectives – rarely the other way round. See also ORGANIZATIONAL LOYALTY.

LPC   See LEAST PREFERRED-CO-WORKER.

Luddite   The term used to describe workers who are obstinately opposed to the introduction of NEW TECHNOLOGY into their workplace. It derives from the followers of Ned Ludd, an early nineteenth century British textile worker, who saw new machinery as a threat to their traditional craft SKILLS and working practices and opposed its introduction violently.

M

Machiavellism   A PERSONALITY characteristic in which a person manipulates others for his own gain. The term is named after the political theories of the fifteenth century Italian statesman and writer Niccolò Machiavelli.

machine controls The knobs, wheels, switches etc. that provide energy or information to a machine.

machine dynamics In ERGONOMICS this term refers to the set of factors involved in the design of the MAN-MACHINE INTERFACE.

machine readable Information presented in such a form that it can readily be identified and processed by a machine.

macroeconomic model In ECONOMICS this is a MODEL of the workings of a total economy.

macroeconomics The part of ECONOMICS that deals with the overall working of an economy and the interrelations between its different factors, including GROSS DOMESTIC PRODUCT and GROSS NATIONAL PRODUCT, EMPLOYMENT and UNEMPLOYMENT, INVESTMENT patterns and national MARKETS. Compare with MICROECONOMICS.

magic thinking Any attempt to understand and manipulate the human condition by recourse to supernatural powers. In particular the term is used to describe the belief that there is a causal link between one's wishes and the real world – that 'wishing can make it so'. It is said to be typical of children, psychotics and 'primitive' peoples but it is not entirely unknown among NORMAL adults in our own society.

Maier's law If the data do not fit the theory, the data must be disposed of. In other words if the facts don't fit your preconceived notion then they're obviously wrong. This was suggested by the American psychologist Norman Maier in exasperation at fellow psychologists' slavish adherence to their pet theories regardless of the evidence. But it is much more widely applicable, of course, than PSYCHOLOGY.

mail order A form of trading conducted mainly through a postal or delivery SYSTEM which connects buyers and sellers.

mailshot An American term for a one-off ADVERTISING circular sent to prospective customers.

mainframe A large, powerful, centralized COMPUTER.

make-work WORK created to keep STAFF or equipment occupied and not because there is any real need for it.

man-machine interface In ERGONOMICS this refers to all those points of contact in the workplace between people and the equipment they use. The term now has a particular reference to INFORMATION TECHNOLOGY.

man-machine system This is at the heart of ERGONOMICS where the workplace is regarded as a SYSTEM within which workers and machines are to be fully integrated.

management 1 Making the most effective use of available resources, whether in the form of machines, money or people. 2 The people responsible for the management of an ORGANIZATION, i.e. for the directing, planning and running of its operations, for the implementation of its policies and the attainment of its objectives.

management accounting The preparation of ACCOUNTING information for use by the MANAGERS of an ORGANIZATION in budgeting, decision-making, PLANNING and formulating policy.

management audit An AUDIT of all aspects of MANAGEMENT in an ORGANIZATION to review the use of all resources and see whether any improvements in efficiency can be made. It includes an examination of CAREER DEVELOPMENT, MORALE of STAFF, the effects of PERSONNEL policies, financial PERFORMANCE, PLANNING effectiveness and the SKILLS of the organization's MANAGERS.

management buyout A situation in which the MANAGERS of an ENTERPRISE make a bid to own it, in whole or in part, by buying out the original shareholders then operating as a separate concern on their own behalf.

management by crisis A MANAGEMENT STYLE that tends to set up crash programmes to deal with problems as they arise in an ORGANIZATION rather than focusing on long-term PLANNING or the overall objectives of the organization. It is a style that suits a MANAGER inclined to AUTHORITARIAN MANAGEMENT and is a way of making short-term CRISIS MANAGEMENT into a permanent arrangement.

management by objectives A term proposed by the American MANAGEMENT specialist PETER DRUCKER in the 1950s to emphasize the importance of setting objectives for – and by – each individual member of an ORGANIZATION as well as the various branches of the organization. Drucker also emphasized the element of self-control and taking responsibility for one's own WORK. As an objective and a quantifiable measure of PERFORMANCE this technique has since become very popular with SENIOR MANAGEMENT, though its application in practice has often been more top down and formalized than Drucker had intended.

management by walking about A technique suggested by some specialists in MANAGEMENT SCIENCE for keeping SENIOR MANAGEMENT, and especially the CHIEF EXECUTIVE, in touch with what is actually happening in the ORGANIZATION. By walking about where people are actually doing the WORK they are able to get information and opinions at first hand and undistorted by passing through the channels of UPWARD COMMUNICATION.

management consultant Someone who offers a CONSULTANCY service in any area of MANAGEMENT or the running of an ORGANIZATION.

management development The process of identifying, TRAINING and generally equipping relatively junior MANAGERS with the experience or SKILL necessary for SENIOR MANAGEMENT positions with an ORGANIZATION in the future. It is a process that, ideally, should be an integral part of a coherent PERSONNEL policy going from initial RECRUITMENT to ultimate RETIREMENT.

management education Any course of instruction in MANAGEMENT and related fields – which is often known as BUSINESS ADMINISTRATION. Success in such a course is usually rewarded with an academic qualification, whether the setting is an institution of higher education or an in-house programme tailored to a particular ORGANIZATION. The term is often used interchangeably with MANAGEMENT TRAINING, though the emphasis of management education is generally more formal and academic.

management game A BUSINESS GAME used in MANAGEMENT TRAINING.

management information system A centralized, and usually computerized, INFORMATION SYSTEM for use by the MANAGERS of an ORGANIZATION in decision-making.

management science 1 The application of scientific methods, and particularly QUANTITATIVE METHODOLOGY, to the practice of MANAGEMENT. 2 The application of a BEHAVIOURAL SCIENCE or SOCIAL SCIENCE perspective to the study of MANAGEMENT.

management service Any service intended to help MANAGEMENT function more effectively, such as DATA PROCESSING or MARKET RESEARCH.

management style The general approach a MANAGER has to dealing with other people at WORK, and in particular the exercising of his or her AUTHORITY with subordinates. This style is often characterized as tending towards AUTHORITARIAN MANAGEMENT or DEMOCRATIC MANAGEMENT, depending on the PERSONALITY of the individual manager, but people can also have somewhat different approaches when faced with different situations. See also THEORY X and THEORY Y.

management training Any form of TRAINING in the practices and techniques of MANAGEMENT. One important form of management training is to have MANAGERS study case histories of real-life issues in ORGANIZATIONS and work on solutions to problems; another is to play BUSINESS GAMES designed to deal with particular aspects of management. The term is often used interchangeably with MANAGEMENT EDUCATION, though the emphasis of management training is generally more focused and less formal or academic.

manager Anyone involved in the ADMINISTRATION of an ORGANIZATION with the AUTHORITY to use organizational resources, whether money, labour, or equipment, in furtherance of the organization's objectives.

managerial accounting See MANAGEMENT ACCOUNTING.

managerial economics The application of ECONOMICS to the kind of practical business decisions that a MANAGER has to take. As well as economics the field draws on OPERATIONAL RESEARCH, MANAGEMENT ACCOUNTING and MARKETING.

managerial grid A technique used in MANAGEMENT DEVELOPMENT that was devised by two American organizational psychologists, Robert Blake and Jane Mouton, building on previous contributions to the study of HUMAN RELATIONS by psychologists like ARGYRIS, LEWIN and LIKERT. The technique consists of scoring managers on two dimensions at right angles to each other to form a grid. The dimensions are *concern for PRODUCTION* (or the TASK in hand) and *concern for people*. Each individual's scores are then plotted on this grid to see how much of each concern they express. The grid also forms the basis for a seminar exploring various aspects of the WORK GROUP. (Fig. 12)

managerial psychology The systematic study of the ROLE of the MANAGER in an ORGANIZATION and in particular the relationships between SUPERVISORS and supervisees. This area of study is a part of INDUSTRIAL PSYCHOLOGY.

manpower analysis An analysis of the employees in an ORGANIZATION that attempts to identify patterns and trends in their EMPLOYMENT. It will examine, for instance, the DISTRIBUTION of employees by age, sex, SKILL, JOB TITLE and length of service. It is the first stage of systematic MANPOWER PLANNING.

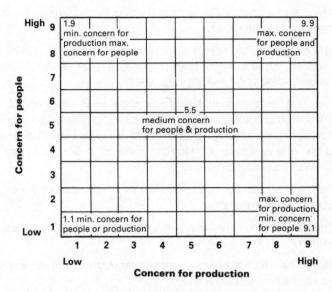

(Adapted from Blake and Mouton, (1964), *The Managerial Grid*)

Figure 12 Managerial grid

manpower audit See MANPOWER ANALYSIS.

manpower forecasting See MANPOWER PLANNING.

manpower planning The process of FORECASTING both the numbers and the kinds of employees that an ORGANIZATION will require over a given period of time and taking steps to ensure their supply. Ideally this should be an integral part of an organization's PERSONNEL policy from RECRUITMENT to RETIREMENT, including SELECTION, PROMOTION, and TRAINING.

manual skill A SKILL that requires physical rather than mental ABILITY.

manual worker Someone employed on the SHOP FLOOR of an ORGANIZ- ATION doing physical rather than mental WORK, whether the work is skilled or unskilled.

marginal cost The extra cost of PRODUCTION of a unit additional to those already produced or planned.

marginality A term used in SOCIAL SCIENCE to denote the effects on an

87

individual or a GROUP of being excluded from the mainstream life of a society. See also DEVIANCE.

margin of error The range of error or inaccuracy usually regarded as acceptable, e.g. in operating machinery or making calculations. See also STANDARD DEVIATION and TOTAL QUALITY.

market 1 A situation where buyers and sellers are in COMMUNICATION with each other. This may take several forms, e.g. in person (as in a cattle auction) or electronically (as in the Stock Exchange) or through the MASS MEDIA as in newspaper ADVERTISING columns. 2 The nature of the demand for a particular product.

market forces The factors determining SUPPLY and DEMAND in a given MARKET. See also PRICING.

market leader The ORGANIZATION with the largest share in a given MARKET.

market niche A unique place or gap in the MARKET for a given product. See also UNIQUE SELLING POINT.

market penetration The amount of demand in a given MARKET that is supplied by a particular ORGANIZATION.

market research Research carried out in the course of MARKETING, either by an ORGANIZATION itself or by SPECIALISTS from an external CONSULTANCY, to determine the likely MARKET for a product or the effects of past or prospective ADVERTISING on consumers. Depending on the kind of information required, the research may use either QUANTITATIVE METHODOLOGY with SURVEY RESEARCH on large numbers of people or QUALITATIVE METHODOLOGY with DEPTH INTERVIEWS of individuals and families and GROUP interviews of 5–10 people in a FACE-TO-FACE GROUP.

market segmentation The analysis of buyers or potential buyers in a given MARKET along various dimensions. These usually include DEMOGRAPHICS like age, sex and SOCIO-ECONOMIC STATUS, buying patterns with respect to price and QUALITY, and PERSONALITY factors like conservatism-radicalism, NEED FOR ACHIEVEMENT or NEED FOR AFFILIATION. The objective is to divide a market into segments comprising similar kinds of people so that MARKETING efforts can be targeted more precisely, and the most effective approach used with each segment.

market share The amount of total demand in a MARKET which a particular ORGANIZATION supplies over a given period of time.

market value The current price that a particular item would fetch in the MARKET.

marketing The series of processes by which demand for goods and services is identified, supplied, anticipated, or manipulated. It relies heavily on such functions as ADVERTISING and MARKET RESEARCH.

marketing concept A philosophy of MARKETING that emphasizes the supreme importance of the customer. Fundamental to this philosophy is an understanding of what the customer wants in any given market, and this is usually ascertained by extensive MARKET RESEARCH.

marketing environment The set of external factors that affect the MARKET in which an ORGANIZATION operates, i.e. cultural, economic, legal, political, geographical etc.

marketing mix The combination of different aspects of an ORGANIZATION's strategy for MARKETING a product, e.g. ADVERTISING, MARKET RESEARCH, PRODUCTION and PUBLIC RELATIONS. The guidelines for the most appropriate mix are sometimes expressed as the 'four Ps' – product, price (market), position and place.

Marx, Karl (1818–1883) A nineteenth century economist and theorist of SOCIALISM who lived and worked (and died) in London and based much of his thought on his analysis of the effects of the INDUSTRIAL REVOLUTION and the British factory SYSTEM. He believed in ECONOMIC DETERMINISM and argued that social harmony and individual happiness lay in changing the economic relationships between people in society, and in particular that labour should not be exploited and workers should own the means of PRODUCTION.

masking In ERGONOMICS this refers to the blocking of one sensory stimulus or process by another.

Maslow, Abraham (1908–1970) An American PERSONALITY theorist and leading exponent of HUMANISTIC PSYCHOLOGY. He is closely associated with the terms HIERARCHY OF NEEDS, PEAK EXPERIENCE and SELF-ACTUALIZATION.

mass media Forms of COMMUNICATION that reach a large – usually nation-wide – audience, i.e. radio, television and newspapers.

mass production The PRODUCTION of identical items on a very large scale. It requires the processes of AUTOMATION, DIVISION OF LABOUR, JOB SIMPLIFICATION, SPECIALIZATION and STANDARDIZATION. In the twentieth century the prototype for mass production was the ASSEMBLY LINE developed in the car manufacturing industry by HENRY FORD. For comparison, see also BATCH PRODUCTION and CONTINUOUS PROCESS PRODUCTION.

massed practice A technique of LEARNING in which the lessons or periods of PRACTICE follow each other without a break. Generally speaking, and for most purposes, this is considered a less effective method of learning than DISTRIBUTED PRACTICE, with which it is usually contrasted.

Master of Business Administration The academic qualification in MANAGEMENT EDUCATION which is generally accepted in the United States as a prerequisite for a professional career as a MANAGER. The qualification is also becoming increasingly sought after in the United Kingdom – but not in other industrialized countries like Germany and Japan which have alternative routes into MANAGEMENT.

maternity leave A period of time off WORK granted to a female employee to have a baby, after which she is entitled to return to her JOB. See also PATERNITY LEAVE.

matrix organization A flexible form of ORGANIZATIONAL STRUCTURE often used in situations which require a mix of people with different SKILLS and experience to be focused on a particular TASK, or an unusual project that crosses existing departmental boundaries in an ORGANIZATION. The people involved in this kind of TASK FORCE will continue to report officially to LINE MANAGEMENT, but in their day-to-day WORK they will be responsible to the project leader.

Mayo, Elton (1880–1949) An Australian psychologist and MANAGEMENT specialist who worked at the Harvard Business School and had a great influence, during the 1920s and 1930s, on the development of INDUSTRIAL PSYCHOLOGY. He is associated particularly with the HAWTHORNE STUDIES which were carried out under his direction. Mayo stressed the importance of HUMAN RELATIONS in the workplace and regarded INTERPERSONAL RELATIONS within the WORK GROUP as the key factor. He encouraged MANAGEMENT to listen to workers on the SHOP FLOOR and take their views seriously – a reaction to the SCIENTIFIC MANAGEMENT advocated by F W TAYLOR, and the dominant industrial image of the ASSEMBLY LINE.

MBA See MASTER OF BUSINESS ADMINISTRATION.

MBO See MANAGEMENT BY OBJECTIVES.

McClelland, David An American psychologist and leading contributor to the study of MOTIVATION. He has suggested that one very important human need is the NEED FOR ACHIEVEMENT, and has provided historical and cross-cultural evidence to support this view. An ENTREPRENEUR will be more concerned with the need for achievement than other people.

McGregor, Douglas An American psychologist and leading contributor to ORGANIZATIONAL THEORY from the HUMAN RELATIONS perspective. He classified the assumptions about human nature made by supporters of the RATIONAL-ECONOMIC view as a rather cynical THEORY X which he rejected in favour of his own, more hopeful, THEORY Y.

MDW See MEASURED DAY WORK.

mean In STATISTICS this is the most commonly used MEASURE OF CENTRAL TENDENCY. It is the arithmetic average, found by summing the values of a series of numbers and dividing this by the total number in the series.

measure of central tendency One of three STATISTICS which can each be used as a central value to describe a series of numbers, the MEAN, the MEDIAN and the MODE.

measured daywork A MANAGEMENT procedure where a daily PRODUCTION target is defined for all the workers on the SHOP FLOOR, whose PAY is then made up of a fixed regular amount for each day that the target is met – as opposed to PAYMENT-BY-RESULTS.

mechanistic organization A term introduced by two British sociologists and MANAGEMENT theorists, Tom Burns and George Stalker. It denotes a relatively closed and formal type of ORGANIZATION with a high degree of BUREAUCRACY, in contrast to an ORGANIC ORGANIZATION.

median In STATISTICS, this is a MEASURE OF CENTRAL TENDENCY which divides a group of scores in half, with half the scores falling above the median score and half below.

membership group In SOCIAL PSYCHOLOGY this term is used to denote the particular GROUP to which an individual belongs. Compare with REFERENCE GROUP.

memory 1 A function of COGNITION which refers to the storage of information. **2** With reference to a COMPUTER, an electronic form of storing information.

mental health Mental and emotional well-being, harmony and INTEGRATION. In the workplace JOB SATISFACTION is crucial to mental health as is the ability to manage STRESS when it arises.

mental set An expectation of, or readiness for, a particular experience.

mere exposure In SOCIAL PSYCHOLOGY, this is a term introduced in the 1960s by the American psychologist Robert Zajonc to explain the phenomenon that, other things being equal, the more familiar people become with objects, words, or pictures of faces they don't know, the more they like them. Mere exposure may thus help to explain the influence of ADVERTISING on buying habits and even political preferences.

merger An amalgamation of two or more organizations into a single new ORGANIZATION by mutual agreement – as opposed to a TAKE-OVER.

merit rating A form of REWARD for members of an ORGANIZATION, based on an assessment of their worth beyond the normally expected PERFORMANCE of their JOB, on the grounds that different people doing the same job can have a different value to the organization. The kind of factors usually taken into account are ABSENTEEISM, APTITUDE, ATTITUDE towards MANAGEMENT, length of service, punctuality, etc.

meritocracy A social SYSTEM in which advancement is based on ABILITY rather than birth or background.

micro Shortened, colloquial form of MICROCOMPUTER.

microchip A tiny piece of silicon, containing a complete electrical circuit, used extensively in the manufacture of the MICROCOMPUTER.

microcomputer A relatively small and cheap COMPUTER that has been designed for specific applications.

microeconomics The part of ECONOMICS that deals with small-scale issues like the prices of individual products, the PERFORMANCE of individual companies, or even a family BUDGET.

microprocessor The MICROCHIP containing the central processing unit of a MICROCOMPUTER. Also used of the microcomputer itself.

mid-life crisis The term applied to the process of reassessing one's personal and WORK life that people typically go through around middle age (from about 35–50). It is inevitably accompanied by ANXIETY and sometimes DEPRESSION.

middle management A MANAGER whose position in the HIERARCHY of an ORGANIZATION is higher than JUNIOR MANAGEMENT and lower than SENIOR MANAGEMENT is part of MIDDLE MANAGEMENT, and this accounts for most managers in most organizations. Middle managers are typically in charge of the constituent units that make up an organization, responsible for the work of other people but with little or no say in the making of policy or the taking of organization-wide decisions.

middleman An individual or an ORGANIZATION acting as a link between others, especially between producers and consumers or retailers, e.g. a furniture wholesaler or a literary agent. See also WHOLESALING.

Milgram, Stanley (1933–1984) An American psychologist who made several contributions to SOCIAL PSYCHOLOGY, particularly in the study of CONFORMITY to AUTHORITY. His best known finding was that most people could be persuaded to give other people electric shocks when told to do so by an authority figure.

milk round The annual visit to institutions of higher education in the United Kingdom by employers in order to make contact with potential JOB candidates.

minimax strategy In GAME THEORY this is the strategy of choosing to minimize loss rather than maximize gain.

Minnesota Multiphasic Personality Inventory For many years this was widely considered to be the leading PAPER-AND-PENCIL TEST of PERSONALITY though it is now somewhat out of fashion. It contains 550 statements which the subject responds to as being true or false about himself. The pattern of responses is intended to reveal certain personality characteristics, particularly those associated with a tendency towards psychological disturbance.

MIS See MANAGEMENT INFORMATION SYSTEM.

mixed economy In ECONOMICS this refers to the kind of economy in which the ownership of the means of PRODUCTION is partly in the PRIVATE SECTOR and partly in the PUBLIC SECTOR.

MMPI See MINNESOTA MULTIPHASIC PERSONALITY INVENTORY.

mnemonic Any trick to aid the MEMORY, such as Every Good Boy Deserves Favour (EGBDF) for the position of notes in a musical scale.

mobility See JOB MOBILITY.

modality In ERGONOMICS and PSYCHOLOGY this term usually refers to a particular form of sensory experience like vision or hearing.

mode In STATISTICS this is a MEASURE OF CENTRAL TENDENCY; the most frequently occurring value in a series of numbers.

model 1 Any representation of an object, situation or ORGANIZATION. It may be physical, verbal, mathematical or produced by COMPUTER SIMULATION. 2 In SOCIAL PSYCHOLOGY it is used of a person whose behaviour is closely observed. See also MODELLING.

modelling In SOCIAL PSYCHOLOGY this is a form of LEARNING from observing a MODEL which goes much further than copying or imitating. Children, especially, may generalize from the model's behaviour to a wide range of similar behaviours of their own invention.

modem From the term 'modulator-demodulator'. It is an electronic device that converts information from a COMPUTER into a form suitable for transmission by telephone, thus enabling COMMUNICATION with other computers.

monetarism In ECONOMICS this refers to the theory that the successful MANAGEMENT of an economy depends crucially on CONTROL of the MONEY SUPPLY, because too rapid a rise in the supply of money can lead to INFLATION.

monetary policy In ECONOMICS this refers to a government's position on the regulation of the amount of spending power available in an economy and the cost of borrowing money, e.g. deciding whether or not to impose a CREDIT SQUEEZE.

money supply In ECONOMICS this refers to the total amount of money circulating within an economy at any given time, whether in the form of notes, coins, bank deposits, etc.

monopoly A situation in which a MARKET is under the CONTROL or domination of a single ORGANIZATION. This condition is generally considered to be met at one-quarter to one-third of the market in question. A monopoly is contrary to the ideal of free trade and is therefore subject to legal sanctions in all industrialized countries with a capitalist or MIXED ECONOMY. Monopolies can occur in both the PRIVATE SECTOR and the PUBLIC SECTOR.

monopsony A situation in which one buyer can CONTROL or greatly influence the price of a product through being the only buyer, or the most powerful buyer, in a particular MARKET.

Monte Carlo methods A technique of SIMULATION, sometimes COMPUTER SIMULATION, that deliberately introduces an element of randomness.

moonlighting Doing a second JOB, usually in the BLACK ECONOMY, in addition to one's normal EMPLOYMENT.

morale An indicator of how much IDENTIFICATION the members of an ORGANIZATION have with its aims and values and how much JOB SATISFACTION they derive from belonging to it.

mores The customs, conventions and practices of a GROUP, an ORGANIZATION, or a society.

motivation In PSYCHOLOGY this is a general term for any part of the hypothetical psychological process which involves the experiencing of needs and DRIVES and the behaviour that leads to the goal which satisfies them. In more popular usage motivation refers to those factors that predispose people to act in one way rather than another. See also HERZBERG TWO-FACTOR THEORY, MASLOW, McCLELLAND and McGREGOR.

motive hierarchy See HIERARCHY OF NEEDS.

motor skill A SKILL that depends on muscular CONTROL and coordination.

mouse The term given to a device designed to make a COMPUTER more USER FRIENDLY. It is a small hand-held box attached to a VISUAL DISPLAY UNIT which is used, instead of the keyboard, to shift the cursor and move text around on the screen.

multimodal distribution In STATISTICS this term refers to a DISTRIBUTION with several MODES.

multinational company A commercial ORGANIZATION which operates in more than one country and moves its resources and activities between them in such a way as to maximize its trading advantages in such areas as labour costs or TAXATION benefits.

multiple-activity chart A CHART which records the activities and interrelationships of workers or machines on the same time scale.

multiplier effect In ECONOMICS this is an idea associated with KEYNES, that emphasizes the powerful effect of even small increases in INVESTMENT.

Murphy's Law   An Irish version of the more general SOD'S LAW.

N

N Ach   The abbreviation for NEED FOR ACHIEVEMENT.

N Aff   The abbreviation for NEED FOR AFFILIATION.

Nader, Ralph (born 1934)   An American lawyer and campaigner whose exposure of shoddy practices in the Detroit car industry of the early 1960s heralded the broad movement of concern for the quality of CONSUMER GOODS known generally as CONSUMERISM.

nationalization   The process by which a state takes over the ownership of a private company or industry and brings it within the CONTROL of the PUBLIC SECTOR. This may be due to practising the IDEOLOGY of SOCIALISM or to the attempt to save a strategic part of the economy from collapse or foreign ownership.

nationalized industry   An industry that has undergone NATIONALIZATION.

natural wastage   The reduction in the number of people employed in an ORGANIZATION through resignation, RETIREMENT or death (rather than a policy of dismissal or REDUNDANCY), who are not then replaced.

near-market research   Scientific research with an evident potential for commercial applications.

need for achievement   A concept associated particularly with the American psychologist DAVID MCCLELLAND. It is the strongly felt MOTIVATION to achieve, to accomplish ambitions and to be successful that is commonly found in the ENTREPRENEUR, for example. McClelland suggested that this motivation is inculcated by careful child-rearing patterns, and especially the encouragement of early achievement (like walking and talking) by mothers – particularly in their first-born sons.

need for affiliation   As used in SOCIAL PSYCHOLOGY this term refers to the need to be with other people, particularly when facing an unpleasant experience. There is some evidence that this need may be related to birth order, with last-born children having least need and first-born children (especially males) having most.

need hierarchy See HIERARCHY OF NEEDS.

need to make sense This is a tendency observed time and again throughout all the diverse areas of PSYCHOLOGY. People apparently have a very deep-rooted need to make sense of themselves, their thoughts and feelings, and of their ENVIRONMENT. This is true whether the environment is physical or social; whether the person is alone in it or with other people. In particular, people are threatened by evidence of ambiguity, disorder or unpredictability and will try very hard to reduce them and feel psychologically more comfortable, even at the expense of the truth. See also COGNITIVE DISSONANCE, EGO DEFENCE and SELF-FULFILLING PROPHECY.

negotiation In INDUSTRIAL RELATIONS this is the essence of the COLLECTIVE BARGAINING process. It refers to the discussion of terms and conditions of EMPLOYMENT by employers and employees, or their representatives, with a view to reaching a mutually acceptable outcome.

neologism Literally, a new word. It is found in scientific and scholarly writing where common words are used in a new way, like BUG or MOUSE, or where new words are concocted like BRAINSTORMING or WORKAHOLIC.

network analysis See CRITICAL PATH ANALYSIS.

network-building Any systematic attempt to link people and resources round a common goal or shared interests and values, like the OLD SCHOOL TIE.

networking Linking people scattered geographically into a single WORK GROUP by electronic means, e.g. TELEWORKING.

new technology The term often used to describe the applied microelectronic devices to be found in the ELECTRONIC OFFICE.

NGO See NON-GOVERNMENTAL ORGANIZATION.

NGT See NOMINAL GROUP TECHNIQUE.

niche marketing The systematic search for a MARKET NICHE usually by a small specialist ORGANIZATION. Its basic principle is the attempt to create a new MARKET rather than increase MARKET SHARE of an existing market.

NIH (Not Invented Here) syndrome The syndrome that militates against copying from, or even LEARNING from, others in the same field. It is usually regarded in MANAGEMENT SCIENCE as a sign of insecurity or inertia masquerading as arrogance, i.e. 'if it wasn't invented here how good can it be?' and was widely used (in the past) by western companies to denigrate the Japanese whose business practices were enthusiastically opposed to the NIH syndrome.

noise 1 Any sound that the listener does not want to hear. Prolonged noise can cause STRESS and even HEARING LOSS, as well as a drop in PRODUCTION. 2 Anything that distracts from the message in a SYSTEM of COMMUNICATION.

Nominal Group Technique Any method for eliciting the ideas of GROUP members on a given topic.

non-directive therapy A form of PSYCHOTHERAPY which accepts an individual's expression of his needs and conflicts on his own terms, without any preconceived system of interpretation for steering the person in a particular direction. Compare with BEHAVIOUR MODIFICATION and PSYCHOANALYSIS.

non-employment The state of neither being in paid EMPLOYMENT nor seeking it – other than being in RETIREMENT, e.g. married women with no paid employment.

non-executive director A director of an ORGANIZATION who is not a full-time employee and who does not have any EXECUTIVE form of AUTHORITY.

Non-governmental Organization This term is usually applied to an ORGANIZATION that operates internationally but is not supported, in the main, by direct governmental funding, e.g. Amnesty International or the Red Cross.

non-parametric statistics Statistical methods that may be used when the data do not conform to a NORMAL DISTRIBUTION, i.e. most data in studies of human behaviour.

non-profit organization Any ORGANIZATION whose ownership resides entirely with its members and whose financial operations are not intended to yield a PROFIT for shareholders, e.g. clubs or neighbourhood associations or charities.

non-verbal behaviour Any form of human behaviour that does not employ speech or writing.

non-verbal communication Direct, face-to-face COMMUNICATION between people by any means other than the spoken word. This would include facial expressions, body gestures, hand gestures, body posture and eye contact.

norm In STATISTICS this is a value representative of a whole set of numbers, such as one of the MEASURES OF CENTRAL TENDENCY (MEAN, MEDIAN and MODE). See also GROUP NORM and SOCIAL NORM.

normal Literally, CONFORMITY to the NORM or standard. As applied to human behaviour it usually refers to what is expected (the SOCIAL NORM) or what is generally considered right, proper, or correct under the given circumstances.

normal distribution The DISTRIBUTION of data from a RANDOM SAMPLE of the POPULATION. When these data are plotted on a graph they show up as a symmetrical BELL-SHAPED CURVE with scores clustered around the average and declining towards either extreme. (Fig. 13)

normative Any behaviour, idea or opinion that pertains to a particular NORM or expectation.

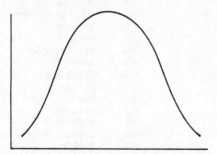

Figure 13 Normal distribution

normative influence In SOCIOLOGY this is the process in which other people's anticipated judgements of right and wrong influence someone's behaviour.

numeracy Literally, the ability to count – the numerical equivalent of literacy. The term is used more widely to include people with no fear of dealing with STATISTICS or mathematics and the ABILITY to handle QUANTITATIVE METHODOLOGY.

O

O & M   See ORGANIZATION AND METHODS.

occupational health   The study of people's health in their WORK ENVIRONMENT, including the factors that contribute to ill-health such as STRESS. This field draws mainly on PSYCHOLOGY and other branches of SOCIAL SCIENCE, as well as medicine. (Fig. 14)

occupational medicine   See INDUSTRIAL MEDICINE.

occupational psychology   Used interchangeably with the older usage of INDUSTRIAL PSYCHOLOGY though strictly speaking it should have a wider remit, covering all occupations regardless of setting.

Miner	8.3	Armed forces	4.7
Police	7.7	Vet	4.5
Construction worker	7.5	Civil servant	4.4
Journalist	7.5	Accountant	4.3
Pilot (civil)	7.5	Engineer	4.3
Prison officer	7.5	Estate agent	4.3
Advertising	7.3	Hairdresser	4.3
Dentist	7.3	Local government officer	4.3
Actor	7.2	Secretary	4.3
Politician	7.0	Solicitor	4.3
Doctor	6.8	Artist, designer	4.2
Taxman	6.8	Architect	4.0
Film producer	6.5	Chiropodist	4.0
Nurse, midwife	6.5	Optician	4.0
Fireman	6.3	Planner	4.0
Musician	6.3	Postman	4.0
Teacher	6.2	Statistician	4.0
Personnel	6.0	Lab technician	3.8
Social worker	6.0	Banker	3.7
Manager (commercial, export)	5.8	Computing	3.7
Press officer	5.8	Occupational therapist	3.7
Professional footballer	5.8	Linguist	3.7
Salesman, shop assistant	5.7	Beauty therapist	3.5
Stockbroker	5.5	Vicar	3.5
Bus driver	5.4	Astronomer	3.4
Psychologist	5.2	Nursery nurse	3.3
Publishing	5.0	Museum worker	2.8
Diplomat	4.8	Librarian	2.0
Farmer	4.8		

Figure 14   Occupational health (a nine-point scale of occupational stress from Cooper, C L, 1985, 'Your place in the stress league', Sunday Times, 24 February, 1985)

occupational therapy An adjunct to PSYCHOTHERAPY in hospitals which involves patients in performing useful TASKS to help improve their SELF-ESTEEM and feelings of worth.

OD See OPERATIONAL DEFINITION.

office technology See ELECTRONIC OFFICE.

off-line That part of a COMPUTER SYSTEM which is not under the immediate CONTROL of the central processing unit and cannot therefore be accessed directly. It is used to produce data that is only required at relatively long intervals, like a monthly bank statement or a quarterly electricity bill. Compare with ON-LINE.

OJT See ON-THE-JOB TRAINING.

old school tie A long-established form of NETWORKING. In this case chaps who went to the same English public school (and are therefore entitled to wear the same tie) practise various forms of mutual aid in later life.

oligopoly In ECONOMICS this is a situation in which a few sellers can CONTROL or dominate a MARKET. Such a situation is widely regarded as an INCENTIVE for the sellers to form a CARTEL. See also DUOPOLY and MONOPOLY.

omnibus survey In MARKET RESEARCH this is a wide-ranging form of survey that seeks to obtain data on many different topics for a number of clients.

on-line That part of a COMPUTER SYSTEM which is under the immediate CONTROL of the central processing unit and can make information immediately accessible to the user by being linked directly to a MAINFRAME and operating in REAL TIME. The most common example is that of an airline seat reservation SYSTEM.

on-the-job training A form of TRAINING that is given to people at their place of WORK, and usually during working hours. In the United Kingdom it often involves SITTING NEXT TO NELLIE.

one-trial learning LEARNING that occurs after a single trial, or practice.

open-plan office A single large room divided into various workplaces but with no fixed walls or barriers between them. It has been associated with a reduction in JOB SATISFACTION.

operational audit See MANAGEMENT AUDIT.

operational definition A definition of something which is based on the operation of the factors which produced it, e.g., INFLATION is defined by the movement of prices and the real value of money. The term is also used more loosely to mean a 'working definition' or a 'rule of thumb'.

operational research A branch of MANAGEMENT SCIENCE that applies mathematics to a series of techniques, like CRITICAL PATH ANALYSIS, which an ORGANIZATION may use in its PLANNING and decision-making. In essence operational research is used to see whether the efficiency and COST EFFECTIVENESS of a SYSTEM can be improved by developing a scientific MODEL to study that SYSTEM, and including within it the factors of chance and RISK.

operations research The American term for OPERATIONAL RESEARCH.

opinion leader A term used in SOCIOLOGY to denote a person of STATUS within a given GROUP whose opinions are highly thought of and who can therefore influence the opinions of other members of the group. See also TWO-STEP FLOW OF COMMUNICATION.

opinion polling A form of SURVEY RESEARCH in which respondents are asked their opinions about goods, services or political candidates.

opportunity cost In ECONOMICS this refers to the last INCOME, PROFIT or time involved in foregoing an alternative course of action, i.e. this is an economic cost and would not be included as an ACCOUNTING cost.

optimization The process of weighing up all the factors in a given situation with the aim of producing the most effective or optimum PERFORMANCE, given unavoidable constraints. Compare with SATISFICING.

OR See OPERATIONAL RESEARCH.

organic organization A term introduced by two British sociologists and MANAGEMENT theorists, Tom Burns and George Stalker. It denotes a relatively open and informal type of ORGANIZATION displaying flexibility in people's JOB DESCRIPTIONS, for example, and encouraging COMMUNICATION and the flow of new ideas outwith the formal CHAIN OF COMMAND. This is in striking contrast to what happens in a MECHANISTIC ORGANIZATION. See also BUREAUCRACY.

organization A GROUP of people brought together for the purpose of achieving certain objectives. As the basic unit of an organization is the ROLE rather than the person in it the organization is maintained in existence, sometimes over a long period of time, despite many changes of members. See also BUREAUCRACY, DIVISION OF LABOUR, FORMAL

ORGANIZATION, HIERARCHY, INFORMAL ORGANIZATION, ORGAN-
IZATIONAL THEORY, and SPECIALIZATION.

Organization and Methods The application of WORK STUDY
techniques to the structure and procedures of an ORGANIZATION in order
to improve the efficiency of the organization's SYSTEMS.

organization chart A CHART outlining the relationships between the
different functions, responsibilities and titles in an ORGANIZATION and
often the people who actually perform them. (Fig. 15)

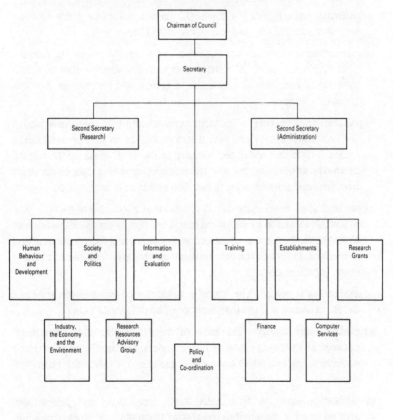

Figure 15 Organization chart

organizational audit An AUDIT of all aspects of an ORGANIZATION's
operations. In practice this is usually the same as a MANAGEMENT AUDIT.

organizational behaviour The behaviour of an ORGANIZATION acting as an entity, rather than that of any individual member.

organizational change The term that describes the process of change within an ORGANIZATION.

organizational climate The ethos of, or commonly perceived feeling about, an ORGANIZATION. It is based on tangible factors like the prevailing MANAGEMENT STYLE, the clarity of goals and values, the time horizons, etc.

organizational conflict A clash of interests, values or goals between individuals or GROUPS within an ORGANIZATION.

organizational convenience A course of action that meets the (usually financial) interests of the ORGANIZATION as a whole rather than the interests of members or customers, e.g. moving to a cheaper, but less accessible, location.

organizational culture This term denotes 'culture' as the term is used in both ANTHROPOLOGY and PSYCHOLOGY, i.e. not only the shared beliefs, values, ATTITUDES and expectations of its members make up the culture of an ORGANIZATION, but also the unquestioned assumptions about its traditions and ways of doing things. See also the NIH SYNDROME.

organizational development A process that affects the ORGANIZATION as a whole as well as its individual members. It involves the application of BEHAVIOURAL SCIENCE to the process of improving the functioning and the MANAGEMENT of the organization, especially in response to changes in the ENVIRONMENT.

organizational goals The formally stated objectives which are the basis for the existence and the maintenance of an ORGANIZATION.

organizational loyalty The basis of the PSYCHOLOGICAL CONTRACT between an ORGANIZATION and its members. It is usually assumed to be something the individual owes the organization – rarely the other way round.

organization man A term, used both approvingly and pejoratively, applied to someone who has the kind of PERSONALITY which allows him to fit relatively comfortably into an ORGANIZATION, particularly a FORMAL ORGANIZATION with some degree of BUREAUCRACY.

organizational pathology Writers on ORGANIZATIONAL THEORY from a HUMAN RELATIONS viewpoint (such as ARGYRIS and McGREGOR) have proposed that an ORGANIZATION can be healthy or unhealthy, just like any of its individual members. Their criteria for judging organizational health parallels accepted criteria for individual mental health, as follows: *Reality testing* – the ABILITY to perceive what is really happening in the ENVIRONMENT and how this is likely to affect the organization. *Adaptability* – the ability to react to a changing environment. *IDENTITY* – the extent to which members are clear on what the organization is, what it stands for and what its GOALS are. Underpinning these criteria is the crucial need for INTEGRATION so that different parts of the organization are not in conflict with each other – a sure sign of pathology in both individual and organization.

organizational politics The games people play when they put individual or GROUP interests above those of the ORGANIZATION as a whole.

organizational psychology Often used interchangeably with the older term INDUSTRIAL PSYCHOLOGY but without the connotation of being limited to ORGANIZATIONS in industrial, or indeed WORK settings.

organizational shape The profile of the levels of HIERARCHY in an ORGANIZATION, the extent to which it is a FLAT ORGANIZATION or a TALL ORGANIZATION.

organizational size The number of members an ORGANIZATION has can have a direct effect on its ORGANIZATIONAL CLIMATE, ORGANIZATIONAL CULTURE and ORGANIZATIONAL STRUCTURE. The larger the number the greater the pressure to operate as a FORMAL ORGANIZATION with a high level of BUREAUCRACY, a relatively fixed CHAIN OF COMMAND, and increased levels in a HIERARCHY of AUTHORITY.

organizational structure The arrangement of the WORK of an ORGANIZATION into the different FUNCTIONAL ROLES and MANAGEMENT ROLES.

organizational symbols Symbols uniquely associated with a particular ORGANIZATION. These may be internal (annual dinner, founder's picture or slogan) or external (LOGO or TRADE MARK).

organizational theory The systematic study of the ORGANIZATION; its structure and functioning and its relationships to the people who comprise it. This area of study draws heavily on PSYCHOLOGY and SOCIOLOGY.

organizational tree See ORGANIZATION CHART.

organizational types Any attempt to classify ORGANIZATIONS along one or more dimensions, e.g. formality, as in MECHANISTIC ORGANIZATION and ORGANIC ORGANIZATION.

outer-directed A term introduced to SOCIOLOGY in the United States in the 1950s by David Riesman to describe people who respond to their society mainly by CONFORMITY to SOCIAL NORMS, by seeking approval and courting popularity. Contrast with INNER-DIRECTED and TRADITION-DIRECTED.

outplacement The process of helping people to find new jobs after notice of REDUNDANCY but while still employed.

outworker See HOME-WORKER.

overachiever A person who exceeds the level of ACHIEVEMENT expected of her. The term is sometimes used in the field of education to describe someone who tries too hard, i.e. a person whose ambitions appear to outstrip her ABILITY. Contrast with UNDERACHIEVER.

overcompensation Producing a greater effort than is needed to overcome a difficulty or resolve a defect. The term is often used in connection with attempts to overcome an INFERIORITY COMPLEX.

overconforming This term is sometimes used to describe a person who is excessively slavish to the demands of AUTHORITY or the conventions of a SOCIAL NORM.

overhead Any recurrent day-to-day expenditure incurred in running an ORGANIZATION other than the costs of labour and material, e.g., rent, heating, and lighting.

overlearning LEARNING in which practice or repetition continues beyond the point required for adequate mastery of the TASK. Overlearning is not usually considered harmful, i.e. it is not thought possible to learn something too well.

overmanning A situation in which there are more people employed by an ORGANIZATION than are necessary for the efficient PERFORMANCE of its WORK. Compare with UNDERMANNING. See also UNDEREMPLOYMENT.

overtime Any time worked outside normal working hours, for which people are paid at a higher rate than the basic level of PAY, usually DOUBLE TIME or TIME-AND-A- HALF.

Owen, Robert (1771–1858) The owner of a textile mill at New Lanark, Scotland in the early nineteenth century, who is sometimes credited with being the first modern MANAGER because he addressed the issues of MOTIVATION and PRODUCTIVITY and was particularly interested in the ATTITUDES of people to their WORK and the MANAGEMENT of that work.

P

pacing The process of allowing a fixed amount of time for the PERFORMANCE of an operation, or an entire JOB, on a moving ASSEMBLY LINE. Usually the time allowed (or pace) is set by machinery under the CONTROL of a SUPERVISOR.

PAI See PERFORMANCE APPRAISAL INTERVIEW.

paired comparisons A method of assessing a series of items and putting them in RANK ORDER by comparing each one with all the others in turn. The method can be used in JOB EVALUATION, e.g. for the PERFORMANCE of a number of MARKET RESEARCH interviewers.

panacea A universal remedy for all problems in an ORGANIZATION. Ideally it should be cheap, painless and change nothing important, which is why *reorganization* is such a great favourite.

panel testing See CONSUMER PANEL.

paper-and-pencil test Any kind of TEST or PROJECTIVE TECHNIQUE that requires written answers.

paradigm A detailed example or MODEL of a particular process.

parameter Mathematically this is a constant in an equation that defines the form of the curve. In PSYCHOLOGY it is a constant that defines the curve of a psychological function like LEARNING. In STATISTICS it takes the form of a measure of a total POPULATION of scores. The term is sometimes used loosely, and wrongly, as if it was 'perimeter'.

parametric statistics STATISTICS that deal with a NORMAL DISTRIBUTION or other POPULATION of scores.

Pareto analysis A technique for identifying and concentrating on the minority of things, both positive and negative, that are thought to contribute most to the operations of an ORGANIZATION. It is sometimes referred to as 'the 80:20 rule', or 'the law of the trivial many and the critical few', e.g. where about 20 per cent of customers account for about 80 per cent of the sales or 20 per cent of stock accounts for 80 per cent of the value of an INVENTORY. It is named after Vilfredo Pareto, the late nineteenth century Italian engineer, economist and sociologist who first suggested the idea.

parity 1 Equal rates of PAY between individuals or GROUPS of people. 2 The perceived fairness of equal rates of pay between individuals or GROUPS of people.

Parkinson's Law WORK expands to fill the time available for its completion. C Northcote Parkinson, the British writer, introduced this concept in the 1950s as a humorous observation but it has since become a serious contribution to MANAGEMENT SCIENCE (like the PETER PRINCIPLE). Parkinson later introduced a variant of his law that is just as familiar in private life as it is in the life of the ORGANIZATION – expenditure rises to meet INCOME.

part method A technique of LEARNING in which the material is broken down into smaller parts to be learned separately and then recombined. Compare this with the WHOLE METHOD.

part-time job Any JOB that takes up less than the NORMAL full-time hours of WORK in any given situation.

participant observation A research technique in SOCIAL SCIENCE where an observer becomes an accepted member of the GROUP he or she wants to study.

participation The term used to describe the involvement of people in the PERFORMANCE of the ORGANIZATION they work for, e.g. by EMPLOYEE OWNERSHIP or PROFIT SHARING.

participative management The kind of MANAGEMENT which emphasizes INDUSTRIAL DEMOCRACY, active worker PARTICIPATION in running an ORGANIZATION and the importance of HUMAN RELATIONS at WORK.

patent A MONOPOLY right, awarded by law to an individual or GROUP, granting sole right to make, use or sell an article or process they have invented. In the United Kingdom a patent normally lasts for twenty years during which time the patent holder is protected from any attempts by others to copy their invention.

paternalism The process of treating adults like children in an

ORGANIZATION by withholding from them any POWER to make decisions affecting their own WORK lives.

paternity leave The male equivalent of MATERNITY LEAVE that may be granted to fathers of new-born children, though for a much shorter period of time.

path-goal theory A type of CONTINGENCY THEORY OF LEADERSHIP which is based on the EXPECTANCY THEORY OF MOTIVATION. It concentrates on maximizing the PERFORMANCE of subordinates in a given situation with the leader or MANAGER having an enabling function of clearing a path for his or her subordinates towards their personal goals at WORK.

Paula Principle This is not a female version of the PETER PRINCIPLE but the inverse of it. It states that women in an ORGANIZATION are held below their level of competence. As the argument behind this principle is that incompetent men are particularly threatened by competent women, it also complements the Peter Principle.

Pavlov, Ivan (1849–1936) A Russian physiologist who won the Nobel prize in 1904 for his WORK on the digestive SYSTEM of dogs. In the course of his reasearch he chanced upon a phenomenon he could not explain and followed it (reluctantly) out of physiology and into PSYCHOLOGY. What puzzled him was that his dogs began to salivate not only when they were presented with food but even before they were fed, when they recognized the man coming to feed them – the essence of CONDITIONING. Though Pavlov thought he had found a way of studying the brain, rather than behaviour, his work inspired a new American school of PSYCHOLOGY called BEHAVIOURISM.

pay An amount of money paid on a regular basis to people in regular EMPLOYMENT. Payment may be of wages or salary, in cash or by cheque or by direct bank transfer.

payment-by-results A SYSTEM of remuneration in which PAY is linked to PRODUCTIVITY. See also PIECEWORK and WORK STUDY.

payment in kind Payment for WORK done in goods and services rather than money.

PBR See PAYMENT-BY-RESULTS.

PC See PERSONAL COMPUTER.

peak experience In HUMANISTIC PSYCHOLOGY this term refers to a rare moment of great emotional POWER in which a person feels something akin to ecstasy, where she is at one with herself and with the world. A moment of SELF-ACTUALIZATION in fact.

pecking order   The HIERARCHY of STATUS relationships formed among farmyard hens by their practice of pecking each other. The most pecked hen has the lowest status. The term is now routinely (and therefore dangerously) applied to status relationships in human GROUPS. Similarly, the term 'hen-pecked' has long been part of everyday speech – though it is applied to males rather than females.

peer group   Any GROUP of people with which one associates on more or less equal terms. It is used of both a social group and a WORK GROUP.

percentile   In STATISTICS, one-hundredth of the total number of scores in a ranked DISTRIBUTION, e.g. the 90th percentile is the point below which lie 90 per cent of the scores.

perceptual defence   The process of defending oneself (one's SELF), or one's EGO, from the awareness of unpleasant perceptions, either by misperceiving them as being pleasant or inoffensive or by not perceiving anything at all.

performance   The way a JOB or TASK is done by an individual, a GROUP or an ORGANIZATION.

performance appraisal interview   An INTERVIEW between an employee and his or her line MANAGER, usually conducted once a year, at which an ASSESSMENT is made of the individual's JOB PERFORMANCE and how it relates to TRAINING needs, PROMOTION opportunities, etc.

performance-related pay   See PAYMENT-BY-RESULTS.

perk   An abbreviation of the word 'perquisite' whose use is largely synonymous with that of FRINGE BENEFIT, although it has overtones of more specific kinds of benefit like free meat for butchers or cheap travel for airline employees. See also PAYMENT IN KIND.

person-job fit   The extent to which the PERSONALITY of an individual fits harmoniously with the JOB she does. On the goodness of fit between the two will depend the crucial factors of WORK like JOB SATISFACTION, PRODUCTIVITY and STRESS.

person perception   The process by which people form impressions of others, then flesh these impressions out and make them more coherent – though not necessarily more accurate. See also NEED TO MAKE SENSE.

personal computer A MICROCOMPUTER used only by a single individual.

personal space In SOCIAL PSYCHOLOGY this is the idea that the area immediately surrounding an individual is felt to be his or her own. The amount of space claimed in this way varies from CULTURE to culture, but any invasion of it is taken as a hostile or threatening act.

personality The sum total of all the factors that make an individual human being both individual and human; the thinking, feeling and behaving that all human beings have in common, and the particular characteristic pattern of these elements that makes every human being unique. Psychologists often emphasize the INTEGRATION and the dynamic nature of an individual's personality and the important ROLE of UNCONSCIOUS processes that may be hidden from the individual but are at least partly perceptible to other people.

personnel 1 The people employed in an ORGANIZATION. 2 The function of dealing with an organization's employees as its HUMAN RESOURCES.

personnel management A specialized function concerned with all aspects of the MANAGEMENT of HUMAN RESOURCES in an ORGANIZATION from RECRUITMENT to RETIREMENT and including conditions of EMPLOYMENT, SELECTION, TRAINING, PLACEMENT, PROMOTION and the WELFARE FUNCTION.

personnel specification See EMPLOYEE PROFILE.

PERT See PROGRAMME EVALUATION AND REVIEW TECHNIQUE.

Peter Principle In a HIERARCHY every employee tends to rise to his level of incompetence – and stick there. Laurence Peter, the Canadian educational psychologist, introduced this concept in the 1960s as a humorous observation but it has since become a serious contribution to MANAGEMENT SCIENCE (like PARKINSON'S LAW). The Peter Principle deals mainly with the experience of men and it has been suggested that there may be a PAULA PRINCIPLE for women.

picket A person or GROUP posted outside their workplace as a TRADE UNION presence during an INDUSTRIAL DISPUTE. The picket will try to persuade other workers to support their side of the dispute by not crossing the picket line and going in to WORK.

pictogram A CHART which uses pictures or symbols to represent numerical data.

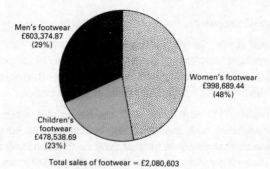

Total sales of footwear = £2,080,603

Figure 16 Pie chart

pie chart A circular CHART with sections representing proportions of some total entity as slices of a pie. (Fig. 16)

piecework A form of PAYMENT-BY-RESULTS where workers are paid for each piece of WORK they do rather than the number of hours they put in. It was based originally on the SCIENTIFIC MANAGEMENT principles of F W TAYLOR.

pilot study A term sometimes used in MARKET RESEARCH or SURVEY RESEARCH, e.g. when a proposed QUESTIONNAIRE may be tested on a few respondents before being used on a large-scale study, to see whether the questionnaire needs revising and whether the study itself is worth doing.

placement The process of placing someone in a JOB, ideally with a perfect PERSON-JOB FIT. This is an important aspect of PERSONNEL MANAGEMENT.

planned economy An economy under the central direction and CONTROL of the state, e.g. under the IDEOLOGY of SOCIALISM, which would decide on matters like PAY and PRODUCTION in the absence of MARKET FORCES.

planned obsolescence See BUILT-IN OBSOLESCENCE.

planning Any attempt systematically to organize the future PERFORMANCE of people or money or goods and services within a given set of constraints and TIME HORIZON.

plant The buildings, equipment and machinery used in the running of an ORGANIZATION, especially in manufacturing industry.

plateau See LEARNING PLATEAU.

pluralistic ignorance   A social situation in which each individual believes himself to be the only exception to the accepted beliefs or behaviour of his GROUP.

point-of-sale advertising   A form of ADVERTISING material that is BELOW THE LINE and placed in retail outlets, i.e. the point at which the sale is actually made.

population   In STATISTICS the total number of cases or individuals from which a sample is drawn for study and about which inferences are to be made.

post-industrial society   A concept associated with the American sociologist Daniel Bell in which the SERVICE SECTOR could become an alternative basis to manufacturing industry for the creation of wealth in society following the adoption of NEW TECHNOLOGY.

power   The ABILITY to make things happen by exerting influence over people or things. The most commonly recognized sources of power are physical strength, knowledge, or position in the HIERARCHY of an ORGANIZATION. But there are also less concrete sources of power such as exist in PERSONALITY factors like CHARISMA or the relationships between people in an organization.

PR   See PUBLIC RELATIONS.

practice   1 In PSYCHOLOGY this term refers to the repetition of certain behaviour during the process of LEARNING some SKILL. 2 In ANTHROPOLOGY and in general usage the term is usually applied to a particular custom or tradition.

predictive validity   See CONSTRUCT VALIDITY.

prejudice   An ATTITUDE, opinion or belief, with a strong emotional underpinning that makes it largely impervious to reason or evidence to the contrary. The term is usually (though not always) used in a negative sense.

presentation of self   A term associated with the Canadian sociologist Erving Goffman who was interested in the way people want others to perceive them. See IMPRESSION MANAGEMENT.

prices and incomes policy   A policy that governments follow whether their IDEOLOGY is in favour of STATE INTERVENTION in the MARKET or having a *LAISSEZ-FAIRE* economy. The object of the policy is to reduce INFLATION and UNEMPLOYMENT and the means of achieving it is to have a reduction in PAY and in prices.

113

pricing The decisions made by an ORGANIZATION in setting a price for the goods or services it provides, taking into account the cost of PRODUCTION and the nature of the MARKET.

primacy effect The finding that, under certain conditions in the process of LEARNING, the first one of a series to be learned is remembered best. See also RECENCY EFFECT.

primary group A small GROUP (such as the family) characterized by direct, intimate, personal relationships between people who depend on each other for support and for satisfaction of emotional needs.

prisoner's dilemma A situation developed out of GAME THEORY and used in SOCIAL PSYCHOLOGY in the study of BARGAINING behaviour. In this particular game two suspects are caught by the police and questioned separately about a crime. If one prisoner confesses and the other does not, the squealer is set free and the fall guy takes the rap. If both confess both are convicted but dealt with leniently. If neither confesses both benefit because they cannot then be convicted.

private sector The part of a MIXED ECONOMY which is controlled by individuals or companies rather than the state. Compare with PUBLIC SECTOR.

privatization The process of transferring the ownership of an ORGANIZATION or an industry from the PUBLIC SECTOR to the PRIVATE SECTOR, usually by the public sale of shares.

privatized industry An industry that has undergone PRIVATIZATION.

proactive inhibition The detrimental effect of previous LEARNING on the recall of later learning. Compare with RETROACTIVE INHIBITION.

probability In STATISTICS this refers to the likelihood that a given event will occur as compared with the likelihood of alternative events occurring. For example, the probability of obtaining a given number when throwing a six-sided dice is one in six.

product cycle See PRODUCT LIFE CYCLE.

product differentiation 1 The packaging and ADVERTISING of different BRANDS of virtually identical products in order to create differences between them in the mind of the consumer. 2 The process of designing and producing a range of the same basic products in order to appeal to different segments of the MARKET, e.g. breakfast cereals with or without fibre, fruit, sugar, etc.

product innovation   A product whose PRODUCTION breaks new ground for an ORGANIZATION, either because of the process involved in producing it or the MARKET it is aimed at.

product life cycle   A term used in MARKETING to describe the different stages that every product goes through from its initial development and introduction to the MARKET, via its initial sales and its established sales, to its eventual decline and withdrawal from the market.

product mix   The range of products, and the particular combination of them at any given time, that an ORGANIZATION produces.

product obsolescence   The final stage of a PRODUCT LIFE CYCLE when it is superseded by other products. Its identification necessitates the withdrawal of the product from the MARKET.

production   All the processes involved in providing goods and services to the MARKET, from the extraction of raw materials to the RETAILING of finished products.

productivity   The rate of output of a worker or a machine.

profession   1 'An occupation possessing high social status and characterized by considerable skill and knowledge, much of which is theoretical and intellectual in nature' (*The Penguin Management Handbook*). 2 'A conspiracy to defraud the laity'. (George Bernard Shaw).

professional socialization   The process of SOCIALIZATION that a new recruit to a PROFESSION has to undergo.

profit   Any financial gain resulting from business activity. It is basically the excess of INCOME over expenditure for a given period of time.

profit centre   A unit of ORGANIZATION which is treated as a separate entity for purposes of financial CONTROL and which is allocated designated INCOME targets which allow its PROFIT to be calculated over a given period of time. This unit may be a department, a place, a person, or even a machine. Contrast with COST CENTRE.

profit sharing   An INCENTIVE involving the DISTRIBUTION of some of the PROFIT made by a business to its employees, over and above their normal PAY, in the form of cash or shares.

Programme Evaluation and Review Technique   The name of a particularly popular technique in CRITICAL PATH ANALYSIS.

programmed learning   A form of LEARNING involving a SYSTEM of self-instruction, based on CONDITIONING, where a TASK to be mastered is broken down into small steps. The subject is given FEEDBACK about his mastery of each step as he goes along.

projection In PSYCHOANALYSIS this refers to an EGO DEFENCE where an individual (at the UNCONSCIOUS level) attributes to other people feelings he has himself but which are too threatening to the EGO to admit into his consciousness.

projective technique A procedure for uncovering an individual's UNCONSCIOUS MOTIVATION, ANXIETY or CONFLICT. Like the RORSCHACH TEST, the 16PF TEST, or the THEMATIC APPERCEPTION TEST, such a procedure consists of presenting relatively unstructured stimuli to the subject, designed to encourage the PROJECTION of material which would be inadmissible to consciousness in a relatively direct and undisguised form.

promotion 1 Any attempt to publicize an ORGANIZATION, its products or its interests, by ADVERTISING or PUBLIC RELATIONS. 2 The process of moving within the same ORGANIZATION to a JOB of greater AUTHORITY, PAY and STATUS.

proprietor The sole owner of an establishment or business.

Protestant work ethic The idea that WORK is both an end-in-itself and a good-in-itself. This was central to the view of society held by leading Protestant reformers like Calvin and Luther. Together with other values they held, like thrift and an emphasis on ACHIEVEMENT, this ethic is widely believed to have been the major contribution to the INDUSTRIAL REVOLUTION and the rise of INDUSTRIALIZATION in the West.

prototype 1 A trial version of a product. 2 The original version of a product as compared to later versions.

psychoanalysis A form of PSYCHOTHERAPY, invented and developed by SIGMUND FREUD. It places great emphasis on the uncovering and understanding of UNCONSCIOUS MOTIVATION. Any form of psycho-analysis, no matter how far removed it may be from its Freudian origins, would subscribe to this principle. Psychoanalysis is the most arduous and demanding form of psychotherapy, requiring years of (expensive) sessions during which a great amount of powerful emotion will be experienced.

psychodiagnostics Any technique applied to the interpretation of PERSONALITY, whether PROJECTIVE TECHNIQUE or PSYCHOMETRIC.

psychodynamics See DYNAMIC PSYCHOLOGY.

psychological contract In ORGANIZATIONAL PSYCHOLOGY this refers to an unwritten (and often unspoken) contract consisting of a set of expectations which the ORGANIZATION and the individual member have of each other. On the degree of fit between these two sets of expectations rests the health and happiness of both.

psychological field See LIFE SPACE.

psychological price The retail price of an item that is generally accepted without question by the consumer, though it may be a relatively high one, largely because of its familiarity. Also known as the CHARM PRICE of an item.

psychological test This term is generally applied very broadly to include any procedure or technique for assessing any aspect of mental or emotional functioning. It would thus include both PROJECTIVE TECHNIQUES and PSYCHOMETRICS.

psychology Most commonly defined at present as 'the study of human and animal behaviour', a definition that accurately describes the route to increasing our psychological *knowledge*. An older definition, 'the science of mental life', focuses on a psychological *understanding* of what that behaviour is about and how to make sense of it most intelligently. Perhaps both these approaches are essential.

psychometrics Those areas of PSYCHOLOGY that deal specifically with the measurement of psychological factors. In a MANAGEMENT ENVIRON-MENT the term tends to be used as a synonym for PSYCHOLOGICAL TESTS.

psychosomatic disorders This term comes from the Greek words *psyche* (mind) and *soma* (body). It relates to psychological disorders in which emotional STRESS produces physiological symptoms. Illnesses such as asthma and stomach ulcers have long been known to be psychosomatic, but it has also been argued that, because of the interrelationship between mind and body, every illness is psychosomatic at least to some extent.

psychotherapy The use of psychological techniques to treat psychological disturbance. The three main forms of psychotherapy are based on the three main theoretical approaches of BEHAVIOURISM, PSYCHOANALYSIS and a broad HUMANISTIC PSYCHOLOGY orientation represented by the work of psychologists like LEWIN and MASLOW.

public administration An old-fashioned term, dating from the time when the systematic study of ADMINISTRATION was considered a PUBLIC SECTOR activity. It has been largely superseded by the terms BUSINESS

ADMINISTRATION (when followed as part of a Master of Business Administration course) and ADMINISTRATIVE SCIENCE.

public relations The systematic attempt by an ORGANIZATION to present itself to best advantage, both to an external public and to its employees, by a process of persuasive COMMUNICATION. It is used in conjunction with paid ADVERTISING and concentrates usually on the MASS MEDIA. The objective of the exercise is to build up and maintain good relations between the organization, its public and its employees.

public sector The part of a MIXED ECONOMY which is controlled by the state rather than by individuals or private companies. Compare with PRIVATE SECTOR.

public utility An ORGANIZATION that provides an essential public service, like the supply of water or electricity, whether it is part of the PRIVATE SECTOR or the PUBLIC SECTOR.

PWE See PROTESTANT WORK ETHIC.

Pygmalion effect A form of SELF-FULFILLING PROPHECY in a social setting that was first suggested by the American psychologist Robert Rosenthal. Rosenthal led a number of teachers to believe that certain children in their classes had high IQs and were expected to do well in the year ahead. The children did do well – though they were all in fact of average IQ. Hence the name Pygmalion from the play by George Bernard Shaw (later made into the musical *My Fair Lady*). The concept has been applied in the world of the ORGANIZATION more widely to describe a MANAGER's expectation of a subordinate.

pyramid hierarchy An ORGANIZATIONAL STRUCTURE having different levels of AUTHORITY with fewer people at each succeeding level, so that a CHART of the HIERARCHY would look like a pyramid in shape. See also TALL ORGANIZATION.

Q

QC See QUALITY CIRCLE.

Q sort A technique for rating different TRAITS of PERSONALITY in which an individual is given a large number of statements about himself, or about someone else, which he then sorts into piles representing the degree to which the statements are applicable.

qualitative methodology The use of research methods in BEHAV-IOURAL SCIENCE or SOCIAL SCIENCE which are concerned more with the complexity and the richness of the data being collected than either the CONTROL of the research situation, the quantity of data generated, or the sophistication of the statistical analysis of them available to the researcher. The open-ended, unstructured INTERVIEW that does not use a detailed QUESTIONNAIRE, and PARTICIPANT OBSERVATION, are probably the most common methods used. Compare with QUANTITATIVE METHODOLOGY.

quality The term is now used mainly as a way of measuring or describing how good or bad a product is at performing its function.

quality circle A technique developed in the 1960s by American and Japanese engineers. Each circle consists of a small local GROUP of employees trying to solve practical problems about the standard of QUALITY of the product they are working on. Membership of the circle is completely voluntary and is seen by MANAGEMENT as a way of improving the PARTICIPATION and MOTIVATION of the work-force, as well as providing the bonus of increased quality and, perhaps as a result, decreased costs.

quality control Any technique, like the QUALITY CIRCLE, for helping to maintain a desired level of QUALITY in the PRODUCTION of a product. Normally this level will be as high as is feasible, but sometimes CONTROL will be exercised to ensure that quality is not *too* high, e.g. in the case of BUILT-IN OBSOLESCENCE. Compare with TOTAL QUALITY.

quality market A MARKET in which the QUALITY of a product is more important to the customer than the price.

quality of working life An approach to WORK that first became prominent in the 1960s. It is concerned to improve the QUALITY of life for people in the workplace by emphasizing the importance of good JOB DESIGN in making work more meaningful for workers and giving them more CONTROL over how they do it.

quango An acronym for a 'quasi-autonomous non-governmental organization' in the United Kingdom. It is an ORGANIZATION which is established and funded indirectly by the government to oversee or encourage activity in a particular area of public interest, e.g. the Economic and Social Research Council or the Scottish Tourist Board.

quantitative methodology The use of research methods in BEHAVIOURAL SCIENCE or SOCIAL SCIENCE which are concerned more with the precision and generalizability of the data being collected than their richness of content or complexity, i.e. having a narrower but sharper focus than QUALITATIVE METHODOLOGY. The experiment and the structured QUESTIONNAIRE are the most common methods used.

quartile In STATISTICS this is one of the three points on a FREQUENCY DISTRIBUTION which divide it into equal quarters.

questionnaire Any set of written questions used in the collecting of information for purposes of comparison. It is widely used in MARKET RESEARCH and is the basis of all work in SURVEY RESEARCH.

queueing In ERGONOMICS this term is used to describe a way of dealing with SENSORY OVERLOAD in which all the stimuli but one are 'put on hold' by the brain until that one has been processed.

quota sampling In STATISTICS this is the process of SAMPLING data from each subgroup of a given POPULATION. This is a particular form of STRATIFIED SAMPLING widely used in MARKET RESEARCH where an interviewer is given a set number or quota of INTERVIEWS to carry out in a given stratum of the population and stops sampling when the quota has been achieved.

QWL See QUALITY OF WORKING LIFE.

R

r In STATISTICS this is the symbol for the most common CORRELATION COEFFICIENT used.

R & D See RESEARCH AND DEVELOPMENT.

racism A negative PREJUDICE against someone of a different race (usually meaning skin colour).

RAM An acronym for RANDOM ACCESS MEMORY.

random access memory The immediately available short-term part of a COMPUTER's memory. Any data sorted in this part is lost when the computer is switched off unless it has been transferred to longer-term memory storage.

random sampling In STATISTICS this is the process of SAMPLING data at random from a POPULATION so that inferences can be made about the population from findings about the sample. The crucial condition is that each individual in the total population has an equal chance of being chosen.

rank order Any series of numbers, items, or individuals arranged in order of magnitude, either increasing or decreasing.

rate setting An old-fashioned term for the process of setting PIECEWORK rates of PAY for a JOB. The process is more often included now under the term WORK MEASUREMENT.

rational-economic A view of human nature which argues that people act only to maximize their self-interest. It is based on the philosophy of HEDONISM and often claims the thought of ADAM SMITH in its support. A MANAGEMENT STYLE which acted on his view would be described as RATIONAL MANAGEMENT. See also THEORY X.

rational management The opposite of PARTICIPATIVE MANAGEMENT. The term is usually used to denote a MANAGEMENT STYLE that emphasizes objective measures of input and output rather than HUMAN RELATIONS.

rationalization 1 In PSYCHOANALYSIS this term is used to describe an EGO DEFENCE in which a person justifies some action about which he has UNCONSCIOUS guilt feelings because he really knows he shouldn't have acted in that way. 2 In ECONOMICS the term is used to denote the application of the most efficient methods in the use of resources in an ORGANIZATION. 3 In ORGANIZATIONAL THEORY the term refers to the creation of a more effective ORGANIZATIONAL STRUCTURE, which often implies one that is simpler and cheaper.

reaction time In ERGONOMICS this term refers to the time elapsed between the presentation of a stimulus and the subject's response to it.

real time A period of time during which an ON-LINE COMPUTER is processing the data about a particular situation while that situation is actually in progress, thus allowing for instant updating, as in an airline or hotel reservation SYSTEM.

real wages 1 Disposable INCOME left after paying TAXATION, etc. 2 The buying POWER of a certain INCOME as opposed to the actual money received.

recency effect   The finding that, under certain conditions in the process of LEARNING, the last one of a series to be learned is remembered best. See also PRIMACY EFFECT.

recession   A lack of growth or a decline in trading or in the economy generally, though not as seriously as in a DEPRESSION.

reciprocity   In ERGONOMICS this refers to the principle that a response is produced by a combination of the duration and intensity of a stimulus.

recruitment   The process of identifying possible candidates for a JOB vacancy. It starts with a JOB ANALYSIS, after which a JOB SPECIFICATION is drawn up. Likely candidates to meet the specification are then trawled, perhaps by ADVERTISING in an appropriate TRADE PRESS or by HEAD-HUNTING. Ideally this process should be the logical outcome of MANPOWER PLANNING and the first stage of a coherent policy of PERSONNEL MANAGEMENT that continues until RETIREMENT.

redeployment   The process of moving workers from one location to another, often with the objective of finding them alternative EMPLOYMENT.

redundancy   The dismissal of someone from his EMPLOYMENT either because his JOB has ceased to exist or his SKILLS are no longer required. See also FIRST IN FIRST OUT, LAST IN FIRST OUT and VOLUNTARY REDUNDANCY.

reference group   In SOCIOLOGY this is the term for a GROUP with which an individual identifies and whose GROUP NORMS he follows, whether he is accepted by it or not and whether he is physically part of it or not. Compare with MEMBERSHIP GROUP.

regression   1 A return by an individual to an earlier form of behaviour. In PSYCHOANALYSIS it is an EGO DEFENCE, where an individual seeks to deal with ANXIETY and avoid UNCONSCIOUS CONFLICTS by reverting to an earlier stage of development where his problems were 'solved' by more infantile means. 2 In STATISTICS the term is used to describe a technique for estimating the relationship between one variable and another. It is applied to FORECASTING, e.g. where qualitative ratings on one variable are used to make quantitative predictions on the other.

reinforcement   The process of strengthening the likelihood that a given behaviour will occur by providing it with some form of REWARD. This is the basis of all CONDITIONING.

relations analysis One of three techniques suggested by PETER DRUCKER to help a WORK ORGANIZATION decide on its most appropriate ORGANIZATIONAL STRUCTURE. This technique is used to establish what the key relations between MANAGERS and all levels in the organization actually are as opposed to unquestioned assumptions about what they are and unthinking reliance on an ORGANIZATION CHART. The other two Drucker techniques are ACTIVITIES ANALYSIS and DECISION ANALYSIS.

relative deprivation In PSYCHOLOGY this term is used to describe an individual's feeling of being deprived when she compares herself to someone else, regardless of the objective reality or what other people may feel, e.g. a managing director might feel deprived with a six-figure salary, if it is less than other managing directors get, while an office junior might be delighted with his own salary which is one-tenth of the figure.

reliability 1 In STATISTICS this term describes the internal consistency of a TEST, i.e. the extent to which it can be expected to produce the same result on different occasions. 2 The extent to which an instrument or a machine or a product provides the PERFORMANCE expected of it over its expected lifetime.

relocation The process of settling an ORGANIZATION or an individual worker in a new place.

reluctant manager A term introduced to MANAGEMENT SCIENCE in the 1980s by two British writers, Richard Scase and Robert Goffee. The term describes a MANAGER suffering from a certain ALIENATION from his JOB because he sees the REWARD for his efforts as being insufficient to compensate him for the STRESS he feels. This reluctance seems to be found more as the amount of BUREAUCRACY in an ORGANIZATION increases.

repetitive strain injury The term sometimes used for a series of injuries to the muscles and skeleton caused by doing repetitive operations on machines for a considerable period of time. It is thought to be particularly prevalent among WORD PROCESSOR users.

representation The procedure where someone acts on behalf of an individual or a GROUP of workers in an ORGANIZATION. Usually this refers to the right of a TRADE UNION to represent its members in dealing with

MANAGEMENT on issues other than those dealing with PAY and conditions of EMPLOYMENT, which are dealt with by COLLECTIVE BARGAINING.

representative sample A sample that is intended to be completely representative of the POPULATION from which it is drawn.

repression In PSYCHOANALYSIS this term is used to describe a particular kind of EGO DEFENCE as well as being a crucial concept in Freudian theory. The essence of representation is the holding back from conscious awareness of disturbing feelings and impulses arising from the ID. They are submerged in the UNCONSCIOUS – where they invariably get up to mischief. FREUD considered repression the price we pay for civilization and psychoanalysis, by making the unconscious conscious, the only way to come to terms with this dilemma. Contrast with INHIBITION.

research and development The first stage of a PRODUCT LIFE CYCLE in which science and TECHNOLOGY is applied to the development of new products. The term is also used more generally to describe any systematic activity within an ORGANIZATION aimed at gaining it a competitive edge in the future.

response bias A MENTAL SET to respond in a particular way to certain issues or questions, e.g., on a QUESTIONNAIRE.

restraint of trade Any activity which interferes with the operation of a FREE MARKET, e.g. price-fixing or preventing a new competitor from entering the MARKET.

restrictive practice This term usually refers to a WORK practice supported by a TRADE UNION, in the interest of JOB SECURITY for its members, which limits the scope of MANAGEMENT, especially in the allocation of particular kinds of work. The practice may or may not be officially agreed through COLLECTIVE BARGAINING. See also CLOSED SHOP, DEMARCATION DISPUTE and OVERMANNING.

restructuring of industry A term often used to describe the decline of HEAVY INDUSTRY, with its attendant UNEMPLOYMENT, and the increasing importance of the SERVICE SECTOR and of INFORMATION TECHNOLOGY.

résumé A French word which is used as an American version of a CURRICULUM VITAE.

retail audit A MARKET RESEARCH technique which involves taking a REPRESENTATIVE SAMPLE of retail outlets and studying them to obtain data on DISTRIBUTION, sales, stock, etc.

retail price index   A figure, calculated monthly, which reflects the cost of a set of basic goods and services used by most of the United Kingdom POPULATION. It is generally used as an indicator of changes in INFLATION and the cost of living and is often the basis for COLLECTIVE BARGAINING and for government policy-making.

retailing   The selling of goods and services, in relatively small quantities, directly to the consumer through a shop or other retail outlet. Compare with WHOLESALING.

retirement   The process of finishing one's full-time WORK life at a designated or generally accepted age.

retirement on the job   A term sometimes used of an employee who experiences such ALIENATION from his JOB that he does the minimum possible in order to retain it while he waits for RETIREMENT.

retroactive inhibition   The detrimental effect of later LEARNING on the recall of previous learning. Compare with PROACTIVE INHIBITION.

reward   Any kind of return (usually positive) as a result of a given behaviour. It is most often used in EMPLOYMENT to refer to monetary gains in return for an individual's PERFORMANCE at WORK. These gains may be in the form of PAY or FRINGE BENEFITS or PERKS.

risk   1 The likelihood, or the statistical PROBABILITY, of failure in an ENTERPRISE; the essence of being an ENTREPRENEUR, and therefore of CAPITALISM. 2 The term is also used of the probability of damage or loss; the essence of insurance.

risk capital   CAPITAL invested in an ENTERPRISE with a high degree of RISK, though usually with the possibility of a large financial gain.

risky shift   In SOCIAL PSYCHOLOGY this term is given to the finding that people will often make decisions of greater RISK under the influence of a GROUP than when they are alone.

robot   A machine which can be programmed and controlled by COMPUTER to function like a person for certain JOBS.

robotics   The study of ROBOTS, their design, manufacture and applications.

role   A term widely used in SOCIAL PSYCHOLOGY to refer to the kind of behaviour expected of a given person in a given situation. The term has been applied generally to the ORGANIZATION and the workplace.

role ambiguity A situation in which an individual is unclear about the ROLE expected of her.

role conflict A situation in which an individual is expected to play two or more ROLES which are in conflict or in competition with each other.

role differentiation The processes of the DIVISION OF LABOUR and of SPECIALIZATION within a GROUP. The larger and more complex the group – from the family to the MULTINATIONAL COMPANY – the greater the degree of role differentiation.

role expectation The expectations other people have about the way a person will play her role in a given situation.

role innovation The process of changing the GOALS and objectives of a particular ROLE.

role model A person after whom an individual will MODEL his/her own PERFORMANCE of a given ROLE.

role negotiation This term is sometimes used to describe a process that may take place during an INTERVIEW with a candidate for a JOB where the exact ROLE the individual would play in the ORGANIZATION is subject to negotiation.

role overload An extreme form of ROLE CONFLICT where the number of different ROLES expected of an individual are simply too great for her to contain. The opposite of ROLE UNDERLOAD.

role playing 1 Acting the part of another person in a therapeutic or BUSINESS GAME situation. 2 Playing a certain ROLE for the particular effect it will cause.

role relationship Any relationship between two people which is defined by the ROLE they each play, e.g. boss and subordinate.

role reversal A situation in which people agree to switch their usual ROLE RELATIONSHIPS, e.g. where army officers serve Christmas dinner to the troops.

role set The SIGNIFICANT OTHERS who have ROLE RELATIONSHIPS with a given individual. (Fig. 17)

role structure The extent to which a ROLE is specified and defined or left open.

role transition The process of switching from one ROLE to another, a process in which SOCIALIZATION is of great importance.

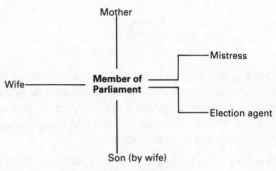

Figure 17 Role set

role underload The opposite of ROLE OVERLOAD. A situation in which an individual feels that her ROLE is not big enough for her. See also UNDEREMPLOYMENT.

Rorschach test The most famous PROJECTIVE TECHNIQUE of all, beloved of cartoonists and comedians. It consists of ten standardized inkblots developed by a Swiss psychiatrist called Hermann Rorschach in the early part of the twentieth century. The subject's responses to the inkblots is analysed by the tester in the light of certain categories that have also been standardized over the years. No diagnosis of someone's PERSONALITY should ever be made solely on the basis of this (or any other) TEST, but many psychologists regard it as a useful first step.

Rosenthal effect See PYGMALION EFFECT.

rote learning LEARNING attempted solely through repetition without any attempt to find order or meaning in the material. Compare with INSIGHT LEARNING.

royalty A fee paid to an author or composer on each sale of published work for which he holds the COPYRIGHT, or to an inventor for the use of an invention for which he holds the PATENT.

RPI See RETAIL PRICE INDEX.

RSI See REPETITIVE STRAIN INJURY.

S

salaried staff This term is usually applied to STAFF who are WHITE-COLLAR WORKERS and whose PAY is calculated on an annual basis and paid in equal monthly instalments. This is in contrast to the BLUE-COLLAR WORKER, for example, who might be paid on an hourly basis or by the amount of WORK completed.

salary structure The arrangement of PAY within an ORGANIZATION such that different grades of employees doing different JOBS will receive different rates. These rates would be based (originally) on the processes of JOB ANALYSIS and JOB EVALUATION, and each would normally be in the form of a scale with annual increments of pay.

sales promotion Any attempt to increase the sales of a particular product by raising public awareness of it through ADVERTISING or PUBLIC RELATIONS.

sampling In STATISTICS this is the process of analysing a sample drawn from a particular POPULATION when it is too difficult or expensive to deal with each member of that population. The most common ways to obtain a sample are by RANDOM SAMPLING and STRATIFIED SAMPLING including QUOTA SAMPLING.

sampling error In STATISTICS this is the extent to which a sample is not an accurate representation of the POPULATION from which it has been drawn.

sampling frame The background or catchment area of POPULATION from which a sample is to be taken.

sapiential authority The idea that the basis for exercising AUTHORITY in certain people lies in their perceived wisdom rather than any formal POWER or STATUS.

satisficing A term that originated in ECONOMICS to describe the situation in which an ORGANIZATION was sufficiently satisfied with what it had achieved to stop striving for more even though it had not reached its ideal or optimal targets. The term is also used more broadly to be almost synonymous with 'compromise' in a situation of CONFLICT where a solution is reached which satisfies all parties but is less than optimal for any of them. See also SUBOPTIMIZATION.

saving face Maintaining one's SELF-ESTEEM or the self-esteem of one's GROUP in a situation of individual or GROUP CONFLICT, or in any kind of BARGAINING. An essential aspect, for example, of successful INDUSTRIAL RELATIONS.

scab An alternative term for BLACKLEG, whose origin is likewise unknown.

Scanlon plan Named after the American TRADE UNION theorist Joseph Scanlon whose plan, first produced in the late 1930s, was intended to herald a new form of co-operative relationship between MANAGEMENT and unions. One outcome of the plan was a method whereby employees would share in the financial benefits of increased PRODUCTIVITY by receiving each month a bonus based on a percentage (usually 50–75 per cent) of savings to the ORGANIZATION in labour costs. The Scanlon Plan is regarded as an important contribution to INDUSTRIAL DEMOCRACY.

scapegoating The DISPLACEMENT of frustration and aggression from its real object, which is too threatening, on to individuals or GROUPS who are unlikely to fight back. The origin of the term 'scapegoat' lies in Biblical times when the Israelites each year sent a pure white goat out to die in the wilderness on the Day of Atonement, symbolically carrying with it all the sins of the people.

scattergram A graph or diagram in which the individual points are left unconnected in order to show what patterns the data falls into.

scenario writing A technique used in FORECASTING where expert predictions about the ENVIRONMENT in which an ORGANIZATION operates are used as the basis for exploring several alternative scenarios for its future development. See also BRAINSTORMING and DELPHI METHOD.

scheduling A term used to describe the process of organizing TASKS to be done by a series of machines in order to streamline PRODUCTION.

schema In the PSYCHOLOGY of COGNITION this term is used to describe a mental MODEL or framework within which new experiences are digested that then allow LEARNING to take place.

Schumacher, Fritz (1911–1977) Generally considered to be the father of the 'Small Is Beautiful' movement in both ORGANIZATIONAL THEORY and in thinking about the global ENVIRONMENT. His work also helped western business theorists to appreciate the Japanese passion for smallness – and with it QUALITY.

scientific management An approach to MANAGEMENT, based on the theories of F W TAYLOR, dealing with the MOTIVATION to WORK. It sees it as a MANAGER's duty to find out the best way to do a given JOB, by a process of WORK MEASUREMENT, then give each worker individual instructions which have to be strictly followed. The individual is thus seen as the extension of his machine, and his REWARDS are also to be allocated mechanically with more PAY expected to produce more output regardless of any other factors. Scientific management is thus the antithesis of the HUMAN RELATIONS approach.

seasonal unemployment A form of UNEMPLOYMENT that peaks at certain times of the year due to the nature of the industry in question, e.g. construction or tourism.

secondary group Another name for a FACE-TO-FACE GROUP.

secondment Moving someone to another JOB or ORGANIZATION for a temporary period.

secretary 1 An individual, usually female, who supports one or more EXECUTIVES in an ORGANIZATION by typing, filing, arranging meetings, screening telephone calls, etc. 2 An individual, usually male, who is the executive responsible for administrative arrangements (and often the legal and financial arrangements) of a GROUP or organization, e.g. the secretary of a golf club, the secretary of a COMMITTEE, or the Permanent Secretary of a government department.

selection The process of choosing someone for a particular JOB, which follows the RECRUITMENT of suitable candidates. The selection process will probably include an INTERVIEW and may also include TESTS of ABILITY, APTITUDE, INTELLIGENCE or PERSONALITY.

selective perception Literally, the process of seeing what you want to see. The process of perceiving the world as we need to perceive it, whatever the relation of that perception to objective reality, is the way we satisfy the NEED TO MAKE SENSE.

self The self, in HUMANISTIC PSYCHOLOGY, is roughly equivalent to the EGO in PSYCHOANALYSIS. It refers to that part of the PERSONALITY which is conscious of its own IDENTITY on a continuous basis over time.

self-activating man The belief that a person can CONTROL his own life to some extent, which is the assumption underlying a PATH–GOAL THEORY of MOTIVATION.

self-actualization According to the American psychologist ABRAHAM MASLOW this term describes the ongoing striving to fulfil one's creative capacities. This is considered an important sign of psychological health.

self-censorship A situation in which people do not say what they really think in a GROUP discussion, for the sake of GROUP COHESIVENESS. This is one of the factors contributing to GROUPTHINK.

self-concept All the elements that make up a person's view of herself, including her SELF-IMAGE.

self-employment Working for oneself and not being a STAFF member of an ORGANIZATION.

self-esteem The degree to which a person likes herself; how worthy she deems herself to be. High self-esteem is generally considered to be an important sign of psychological health.

self-fulfilling prophecy The idea that expectations concerning one's own or other people's behaviour can lead to the expected behaviour appearing, such as in the PYGMALION EFFECT.

self-image The SELF a person believes himself to be. One's self-image is a composite of many things and may bear little relation to any objective ASSESSMENT of oneself or the assessment of others. It begins very early in life and is probably, to a large extent, physical. This early body image can stay with a person for the rest of his life. The judgements of other people are also important in the formation of the self-image, but even though someone's social contacts, and therefore the judgements made of him, may change greatly in later life, he may still think of himself in terms of the earlier judgements.

self-knowledge Having an accurate awareness of what our SELF is really like. Where such knowledge is painful we will invest an enormous amount of energy in *not* knowing. See also EGO DEFENCE.

seller's market A MARKET situation in which sellers have more POWER to influence prices and conditions of sale than buyers, usually because demand exceeds supply. Always contrasted with BUYER'S MARKET.

selling 1 The process of exchanging goods or services for money. 2 The functions in an ORGANIZATION which are most concerned with this process. These now include ADVERTISING, DISTRIBUTION, MARKETING and QUALITY CONTROL as well as sales and SALES PROMOTION.

senior management The term applied to MANAGERS who are relatively high in the HIERARCHY of an ORGANIZATION because they are senior in level of responsibility and AUTHORITY, and often in age as well.

seniority   This term refers either to higher rank or greater length of service in an ORGANIZATION.

sensitivity training   A technique for trying to improve interpersonal COMMUNICATION and the QUALITY of INTERPERSONAL RELATIONS in small groups. The orientation of this technique is that of HUMANISTIC PSYCHOLOGY and it is based on the methods and experience of GROUP THERAPY. Group leaders try to facilitate open and honest discussion of feelings within the group. The hope is that any new-found sensitivity to one's dealings with other people will carry over to other areas of life, such as WORK GROUPS.

sensory deprivation   A situation in which people are deprived of the usual stimulation their senses encounter in daily life. Apparently when people are isolated from sensory stimulation, as far as possible, in a laboratory, they quickly become bored and then start to hallucinate. It may be that when we have nothing in our ENVIRONMENT for our brains to work on and make sense of, we feel a need to provide our own sensations and make sense out of nothing. Something similar seems to happen in particularly monotonous and boring JOBS. Compare with SENSORY OVERLOAD.

sensory overload   The opposite problem to SENSORY DEPRIVATION, where there is so much stimulation of the senses that the brain cannot process them all and 'shuts down' in self-defence.

serial learning   The process of LEARNING material in a particular order or sequence.

service sector   That sector of a MIXED ECONOMY which is concerned not with the conversion of raw materials or the PRODUCTION of goods but with providing a service, such as ADVERTISING, education, health or transport.

servomechanism   A SYSTEM that has CONTROL over another system. FEEDBACK from the system under control enables the servomechanism to regulate its input so that a constant output is maintained. A thermostat is the usual example given of a servomechanism but HOMEOSTASIS in the body can also be seen in this way.

severance pay   A payment made to an employee either because his contract of EMPLOYMENT has ended or because he has to lose his JOB through no fault of his own, e.g. REDUNDANCY.

sex differences These refer to all differences in behaviour or ABILITY between males and females. As with supposed racial differences there is no evidence that there are any. What looks like a genetic sex difference in aggressiveness, for instance, is due to a cultural process of LEARNING the SEX ROLE considered appropriate for either males or females. See also SEX-LINKED TRAIT.

sex-linked trait A genetically transmitted TRAIT which is found more frequently in one sex than the other. A relatively rare occurrence. Perhaps the clearest example is that of red-green COLOUR BLINDNESS which is far more common in men than women.

sex role The different behaviour a society expects of a male or female person on the basis of their sex. As social differences invariably implies PREJUDICE, this is the basis for SEXISM in society.

sexism A negative PREJUDICE against someone on the basis of their sex. Usually by men against women.

sexual harassment The occurrence of verbal or physical abuse solely on the basis of the sex of the victim. It is very common in the workplace and almost always by men against women.

shadow price Computerese for OPPORTUNITY COST.

shelf-life The amount of time a product has before it starts to deteriorate. See also BUILT-IN OBSOLESCENCE.

shift work The process of dividing the whole 24-hour day into WORK periods, often of eight hours each, e.g. midnight–8.00 a.m., 8.00 a.m.– 4.00 p.m., and 4.00 p.m.–midnight. Shift work is used to obtain maximum use of PLANT in manufacturing, or of the work-force in the SERVICE SECTOR, especially that part of it which includes the emergency services where continuous cover is required.

shop floor A term originally applied to the area of a factory in which PRODUCTION took place. It has been widened in its application to indicate the BLUE-COLLAR WORKERS in an ORGANIZATION as opposed to the WHITE-COLLAR WORKERS, or even the work-force in general as opposed to the MANAGEMENT.

shop steward A TRADE UNION official elected by fellow workers on the

SHOP FLOOR to represent them in their day-to-day dealings with the employers or their MANAGEMENT representatives.

short-time working A situation in which a workplace is forced to WORK a reduced working week because of a shortage of orders. This is seen as a temporary measure to cut labour costs while retaining the work-force intact.

shortlist A list of the leading candidates for a particular JOB as the result of a RECRUITMENT process. People on the shortlist will be asked to attend an INTERVIEW, and will perhaps be given some TESTS as well, before the final SELECTION is made.

sick building syndrome This term was introduced in the late 1980s to describe relatively minor but frequent ailments (like sore throats, headaches or eyestrain) that are attributed to factors in the workplace ENVIRONMENT. It is thought that inadequate lighting and ventilation, combined with a closed, automated physical environment over which workers have no CONTROL, are at the root of the syndrome. It is seen as another instance of workers fitting themselves into an old TECHNOLOGY and suffering from it while NEW TECHNOLOGY is applied only for the benefit of machines.

sick pay PAY given to workers who are off WORK for reasons of illness or injury. As well as statutory provisions there are many occupational schemes and these are sometimes regarded as a FRINGE BENEFIT of a JOB.

sickness benefit See SICK PAY.

signal detection theory In ERGONOMICS this theory suggests that the perception (or detection) of a given stimulus (or signal) is related to the sensitivity of the sense receptors (eyes, ears, etc.) and the MOTIVATION of the individual to respond.

significant other A term introduced to SOCIAL SCIENCE in the 1920s by the American sociologist G H Mead to denote a person who is particularly important to us, especially in the support of our SELF-IMAGE. This term is usually compared with GENERALIZED OTHER.

SIMO chart In ERGONOMICS the Simultaneous Motion Cycle Chart is used to record and CHART the co-ordination of workers' limb movements or THERBLIGS. It is one of the techniques of WORK MEASUREMENT invented by FRANK GILBRETH.

simulation The creation of a controlled replication of a real-life situation for purposes of TRAINING, analysis or policy decision-making. It may be abstract and use sophisticated mathematics (like a simulation, or MODEL, of the world economy) or concrete and use the BUSINESS GAME.

sinecure   Paid EMPLOYMENT with little or no WORK attached to it, i.e. even less than in the case of UNDEREMPLOYMENT.

sitting next to Nellie   The traditional form of ON-THE-JOB TRAINING on the British SHOP FLOOR where the trainee learned the JOB by observing and emulating the highly experienced 'Nellie'.

16PF test   This is a PSYCHOLOGICAL TEST of PERSONALITY, developed by the American psychologist Raymond Cattell, which attempts to measure sixteen major personality factors (hence 16PF). The test is sometimes used in OCCUPATIONAL PSYCHOLOGY for the purpose of SELECTION where the findings are matched against important personality factors that have been identified for various occupations.

skill   A learned response, often as the result of specific TRAINING, which affords someone the ABILITY to perform a particular TASK and achieve a particular GOAL.

skills analysis   A part of JOB ANALYSIS.

Skinner, B F (1904–1990)   An American psychologist and the most celebrated exponent of BEHAVIOURISM, not just in the study of PSYCHOLOGY but as a means of running a society. His own technique of CONDITIONING was based on the research of PAVLOV and WATSON. In recent years he has expounded the social implications of his views in a number of influential works intended for the general public.

sleep deprivation   The lack of a usual amount of sleep over a given period of time. This is an area of particular interest in the study of the effects of SHIFT WORK or jet travel on PERFORMANCE. When people are prevented from sleeping they eventually experience ill effects such as hallucinations and confusions of thought and behaviour. Some scientists engaged in dream research argue that dreaming is the most important aspect of sleeping and sleep deprivation. Indeed other than dreaming it is difficult to detect any physiological difference between sleeping and just resting. Note also the similarities to SENSORY DEPRIVATION.

sleeper effect   A term used in several different senses in the SOCIAL PSYCHOLOGY of ATTITUDE change. 1 Its most frequent usage is probably in describing a change in an attitude or opinion after a study has been conducted. This may be one reason for inaccuracy in public opinion polls. **2** The term is also used to describe a more favourable response to a COMMUNICATION after some time has elapsed, rather than the expected decline in the effect of the communication. **3** Sleeper effect is also used to describe the dissociation between communication and communicator over time so that people may become less receptive to positive sources and more receptive to negative ones.

Sloan, Alfred P (1875–1966) An American industrialist who took over a small and ailing motor manufacturer, General Motors, in the early 1920s and turned it into one of the biggest corporations in the world – and at the expense of the Ford Motor Company. He did so mainly by introducing the concept of professional MANAGEMENT to a business world that was still largely run by the personal PROPRIETOR, like HENRY FORD, whose company almost went out of business in competition with GM.

slush fund An informal, unofficial and sometimes dubious source of funds from which an ORGANIZATION can finance a great variety of informal, unofficial and sometimes dubious activities, ranging from STAFF outings to bribing public officials.

Smith, Adam (1723–1790) An eighteenth century Scottish economist and philosopher who based his doctrines of the FREE MARKET on a RATIONAL-ECONOMIC view of human nature. He argued that, as individual self-interest was the driving force whose aggregate effects resulted in social harmony, there should therefore be no state intervention in the MARKET between buyers and sellers. He also proposed SPECIALIZATION and the DIVISION OF LABOUR in manufacturing.

social accounting A particular concern with the social aspects of a COST-BENEFIT ANALYSIS.

social anthropology The systematic study of the SOCIAL SYSTEM and the CULTURE of different societies, particularly non-literate societies. Its major research method is PARTICIPANT OBSERVATION.

social audit As SOCIAL ACCOUNTING.

social class A rather old-fashioned term for SOCIO-ECONOMIC STATUS. Considered crude and gauche in some quarters, if not downright subversive.

social cohesion A similar process to that of GROUP COHESIVENESS, though on a larger scale extending to an entire CULTURE or society.

social comparison The process of evaluating one's ATTITUDES and behaviour by comparing them with those of other people. In SOCIAL PSYCHOLOGY there is an idea that when people are uncertain of what to do (or think or feel) in a given situation they are more likely to take their cue from other people and conform to their behaviour.

social contact See INTERPERSONAL CONTACT.

social control The CONTROL that a GROUP, or CULTURE, or society exerts upon the individuals who comprise it. This control stems from the process of SOCIALIZATION and is exhibited as CONFORMITY pressures towards SOCIAL NORMS.

social costs The data for SOCIAL ACCOUNTING.

social Darwinism The application to human society of Charles Darwin's theories of natural selection, where only the fittest members of a species survive because of their successful adaptation to the ENVIRONMENT. In effect it was in Victorian times (and still is) an attempt to justify the existing order by arguing that the rich and successful have evidently been selected by nature to be rich and successful – the corollary being that the poor are meant to be poor. In practice it becomes a SELF-FULFILLING PROPHECY.

social deprivation In SOCIOLOGY this term is used to describe the situation of an individual or GROUP lacking the material benefits which are generally enjoyed in a society. Compare with RELATIVE DEPRIVATION.

social distance The degree of social intimacy someone will accept in relation to other individuals or GROUPS.

social-emotional leader The individual who may emerge in a small GROUP as the person who keeps up the morale and facilitates the INTERPERSONAL RELATIONS of the group. Compare with TASK LEADER.

social facilitation The stimulating effect on someone's behaviour of other people – even the mere presence of other people. The HAWTHORNE EFFECT is an example of social facilitation.

social influence A basic concept of SOCIAL PSYCHOLOGY which refers to the effects on a person of relations with others, whether individuals, GROUPS, or society in general.

social interaction The mutual SOCIAL INFLUENCE that people have on each other's behaviour in a social setting.

social norm Behaviour that is expected of all the members of a society. The NORM of social behaviour is therefore one way of defining social normality.

social psychology The branch of PSYCHOLOGY that deals with social life, the behaviour of people in GROUPS, and the behaviour of individuals in social settings.

social science Any field of study concerned with people as social beings. To a greater or lesser extent these are generally considered to include ANTHROPOLOGY, ECONOMICS, history, political science, PSYCHOLOGY and SOCIOLOGY. Compare with BEHAVIOURAL SCIENCE.

social skills A set of SKILLS in dealing with other people which determine someone's effectiveness in a social or GROUP setting. They include INTERPERSONAL SKILLS DEVELOPMENT as well as INTERPERSONAL RELATIONS and NON-VERBAL COMMUNICATION.

social status Someone's general position in society in relation to, and as determined by, other people.

social stratification In SOCIOLOGY this term refers to the division of a society into a series of strata of differing SOCIAL CLASS or SOCIO-ECONOMIC STATUS.

social support Positive INTERPERSONAL RELATIONS with colleagues, friends or family which are particularly helpful in dealing with the effects of STRESS.

social system Any set of ROLE RELATIONSHIPS or INTERPERSONAL RELATIONS, from a couple to the entire planet.

socialism An economic SYSTEM characterized by state ownership of the means of PRODUCTION and DISTRIBUTION.

socialization The process whereby an individual becomes a social being. Although it is a lifetime process it is particularly important in childhood when society is represented by (and through) a child's parents and the rest of her family. See also PROFESSIONAL SOCIALIZATION. (Fig. 18)

socio-economic status In SOCIOLOGY this term refers to the categories produced from the SOCIAL STRATIFICATION of a society by INCOME and occupation. In the United Kingdom these are six in number and they are widely used in ADVERTISING, MARKET RESEARCH and SURVEY RESEARCH:

A (upper middle class)
   higher managerial, administrative or professional
B (middle class)
   intermediate managerial, administrative or professional

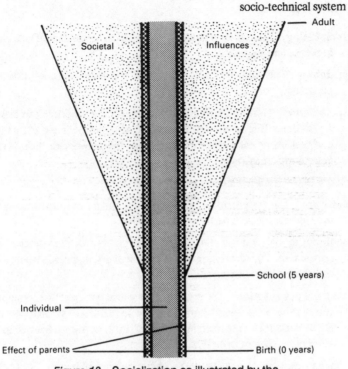

Figure 18 Socialization as illustrated by the
Statt Cone

C1 (lower middle class)
   supervisory, clerical, junior managerial, administrative or professional
C2 (skilled working class)
   skilled manual workers
D (working class)
   semi-skilled and unskilled workers
E (lowest level of subsistence)
   state pensioners, widows, casual and lowest grade workers.

socio-technical system In ERGONOMICS this term is used to describe a
   SYSTEM combining social and technical factors that underlie the interaction of people and machines in an ORGANIZATION. It emerged from the
   approach to MANAGEMENT of the Tavistock Institute of HUMAN
   RELATIONS in London, led by ERIC TRIST. The objective of this approach
   was to jointly optimize TASK PERFORMANCE and JOB SATISFACTION.

sociobiology The study of the possible biological bases of social behaviour in people and animals.

sociology The study of society in general and social ORGANIZATION in particular.

sociometry A term and a technique invented by the American psychiatrist J L Moreno. It is an attempt to measure what people in a GROUP think and feel about each other by setting out the network of their INTER-PERSONAL RELATIONS.

Sod's Law If something can go wrong, it will.

software The COMPUTER PROGRAMS, codes and other support materials available for use with particular HARDWARE.

somatizing A term sometimes used in PSYCHOTHERAPY to describe the appearance of physical symptoms as a result of psychological STRESS, as in PSYCHOSOMATIC DISORDERS.

sour grapes reaction The process of convincing yourself that something you can't have is not worth having anyway. In CLINICAL PSYCHOLOGY this is called RATIONALIZATION; in SOCIAL PSYCHOLOGY it is regarded as an attempt to resolve COGNITIVE DISSONANCE.

spaced practice Any LEARNING with a time interval between PRACTICE but which does not necessarily distribute the practice to maximum advantage in the time available, as does DISTRIBUTED PRACTICE.

span of control The number of subordinates who report directly to a given MANAGER and over whose WORK he exercises AUTHORITY. Generally speaking, the higher a manager is in the HIERARCHY of an ORGANIZATION the smaller the span of control he has to deal with.

SPC See STATISTICAL PROCESS CONTROL.

specialist An individual who is an expert in one particular field of study, or in the use of a certain ABILITY or SKILL, or even in the PERFORMANCE of a particular TASK.

specialization In ECONOMICS this term refers to part of the DIVISION OF LABOUR in which a given TASK is broken down as far as possible into subtasks, each of which then becomes the responsibility of a SPECIALIST worker. Specialization is therefore an important basis for MASS PRODUCTION.

speech processing The capacity of a COMPUTER to recognize and react to the spoken word.

split shift In SHIFT WORK practice this term refers to a shift which has been divided into two or more periods of time and/or GROUPS of workers.

spontaneous recovery In CONDITIONING this term refers to the reappearance of a conditioned response which had been extinguished, after a short rest period.

spreadsheet A technique, that originated in ACCOUNTING, for displaying items in a wide series of columns (i.e. on a spread sheet of paper) so that calculations could be made by row or column as well as by item. The term has now largely been taken over by the COMPUTER world to refer to SOFT-WARE packages that produce spreadsheets for VISUAL DISPLAY UNITS from which rapid electronic calculations can be made.

SPSS An acronym for Statistical Package for Social Science which is a SOFTWARE package for the statistical analysis of SURVEY RESEARCH data in SOCIAL SCIENCE.

SQC See STATISTICAL QUALITY CONTROL.

stability zones A term introduced in 1970 by the American futurologist Alvin Toffler to describe those relationships, times, and places in busy lives, that are otherwise full of STRESS, which provide essential oases of calm and continuity. These can range from a long-term supportive marriage to half an hour's daily meditation.

staff This term is most often used to describe the WHITE-COLLAR WORKERS – usually full-time employees – of an ORGANIZATION, as opposed to BLUE-COLLAR WORKERS. The term often refers to a difference of STATUS in term of PAY, conditions of EMPLOYMENT and FRINGE BENEFITS.

staff appraisal The ASSESSMENT of how well a member of STAFF is doing. It is usual to include a PERFORMANCE APPRAISAL INTERVIEW as part of this process.

staff association In terms of INDUSTRIAL RELATIONS a staff association is equivalent to a COMPANY UNION as it usually has no powers of COLLECTIVE BARGAINING on PAY and conditions of EMPLOYMENT. It also has the function of organizing social activities for STAFF.

staff inspection A JOB ANALYSIS of all STAFF positions in an ORGANIZATION as the first step in a process of RATIONALIZATION.

staff management 1 The MANAGEMENT of STAFF in an ORGAN-

IZATION. **2** MANAGERS who have a SPECIALIST service or advisory support function and are not in the CHAIN OF COMMAND of the organization's HIERARCHY.

staff turnover See LABOUR TURNOVER.

stagflation In ECONOMICS this term is used to describe a situation which combines stagnation with INFLATION, where output and consumer demand are static though prices are rising.

standard deviation In STATISTICS this is a measure of the dispersion or variability of the scores in a DISTRIBUTION. It is the square root of the mean of the squares of each deviation from the MEAN. Or, to put it simply, it is the average distance of each score from the mean.

standard error of the mean In STATISTICS this is the STANDARD DEVIATION of the theoretical SAMPLING DISTRIBUTION of the MEAN, or the extent to which the mean obtained differs from the true mean of the POPULATION from which the sample was taken.

standard hour In WORK STUDY this term refers to a unit of WORK rather than time. It is the measure of the PERFORMANCE of a standard operator for a given TASK over one hour.

standardization **1** The process of PRODUCTION that provides standard machine parts through a wide variety of manufacturing. This is one of the bases of MASS PRODUCTION. **2** The process of setting generally acceptable standards of product QUALITY.

state intervention The intervention by government, either directly or indirectly, in the workings of the economy.

state-of-the-art The very latest product in its field.

statistical process control The use of statistical techniques to determine the acceptable limits of variation in output on a given process, and to correct the process if the output falls outside these limits.

statistical quality control The use of statistical techniques to determine the acceptable limits of variation in QUALITY of a given product, usually involving RANDOM SAMPLING of the output.

statistical significance In STATISTICS this term refers to the PROBABILITY that the results in question could have occurred by chance alone. The highest probability acceptable to current convention is 5 in 100, or a 0.05 level of significance.

statistics A form of mathematics used on data gathered in studying behaviour and by which investigators evaluate their findings and make inferences of wider implication than their study sample.

Statt's Saw There is an exception to every rule, including this one.

status **1** The standing of an individual in an ORGANIZATION. This is based on the amount of respect he is accorded by other people, whether it is because of his position in the HIERARCHY or because of personal qualities like CHARISMA. **2** The standing of a document under discussion. How formal or official is it and what is the appropriate way of responding to it?

status symbol A measure of someone's STATUS and importance (or sometimes self-importance) in an ORGANIZATION. Favourite status symbols are dress (e.g. 'white collar' as opposed to blue) and offices and office furnishings (the size, position and furnishings of an office are often a finely calibrated guide to the occupant's status, both in the HIERARCHY and in the importance attached to his function).

steady state A term used by the British writer on ORGANIZATIONAL THEORY, Charles Handy, to characterize the routine day-to-day activities of an ORGANIZATION that keep it going and which account for about 80 per cent of its WORK. See also PARETO ANALYSIS.

stereotype In PSYCHOLOGY this term denotes an oversimplified perception of some aspect of the social world. This often tends to be a basis for PREJUDICE.

strain The effect of exceptionally heavy demands being placed on an individual or SYSTEM. Often used interchangeably with STRESS, but where a distinction is made strain tends to be regarded as a preliminary to, or a symptom of, stress.

strategic planning The basis of a CORPORATE PLAN or other broad-based and long-term assessment of an ORGANIZATION's future.

stratified sampling In STATISTICS, this is a technique frequently used for mass OPINION POLLING. It involves the division of a POPULATION into subgroups or strata and then taking a RANDOM SAMPLE of each one.

stress Physical and psychological tension and STRAIN, usually accumulated over a period of time, which threatens a person's ABILITY to go on coping with the demands of a given situation. If it is not dealt with it will frequently result in PSYCHOSOMATIC DISORDERS.

stress interview An INTERVIEW that is deliberately conducted by the interviewer in a harsh and hostile manner with the supposed intention of testing the interviewee. It is more likely to be the sign of a man with an INFERIORITY COMPLEX testing his manhood.

strike The ultimate form of INDUSTRIAL ACTION by employees in dispute with their employers, where they withhold their labour until the dispute is settled.

Strong–Campbell Interest Inventory The 1974 revised version of the 1927 STRONG VOCATIONAL INTEREST BLANK which takes account of nearly half a century of history in the world of WORK and the concomitant vocational and occupational changes.

Strong Vocational Interest Blank A QUESTIONNAIRE about a person's interests which is matched with the reported interests of people in different vocations to assess their suitability for a particular kind of WORK. This TEST was first developed in 1927 and revised in 1974 as the STRONG-CAMPBELL INTEREST INVENTORY.

structural change Deep-seated changes that affect the very structure of a society, like the INDUSTRIAL REVOLUTION

structural unemployment UNEMPLOYMENT that arises from the changing structure of an industry or society (e.g. in the pattern of demand) that is long term or even permanent, as opposed to SEASONAL UNEMPLOYMENT or unemployment that is a temporary reflection of prevailing economic conditions.

structuralism A school of PSYCHOLOGY which emphasizes the contents of the mind as it appears to introspection and the mental framework, or structure, that contains these contents. Contrast with FUNCTIONALISM.

structured interview An INTERVIEW in which the interviewee is led through a fixed series of topics based on a set of prepared questions, often raised in a particular order. This method emphasizes comparability of respondents at the expense of flexibility for the interviewer and scope for amplifying answers by the interviewee. Compare with UNSTRUCTURED INTERVIEW.

subcontracting The practice of making an agreement between the main contractor responsible for a project and another ORGANIZATION which will subcontract to carry out part of the WORK on it.

subculture A term borrowed from ANTHROPOLOGY by SOCIOLOGY to denote a CULTURE within a culture, i.e. one which shares most of the main features and values of the parent culture while retaining special characteristics of its own.

sublimation In PSYCHOANALYSIS this is an EGO DEFENCE in which unacceptable UNCONSCIOUS impulses are channelled into consciously acceptable forms. For FREUD this was society's main way of handling REPRESSION. It is certainly the most socially acceptable of the ego defences and may be the source of energy of the WORKAHOLIC, for instance.

subliminal advertising The term 'subliminal' in PSYCHOLOGY refers to sensory stimulation – in this case the presentation of an image – below the 'limen' or threshold above which perception becomes conscious. Subliminal ADVERTISING would therefore mean that the viewer of a film or television message would not be conscious of seeing it – and therefore, it is argued, not conscious of being persuaded. For this reason such advertising is banned in most countries, although there is no firm evidence that subliminal perception actually has any effect. However, there may not really be a problem; many psychologists believe that subliminal perception is impossible.

suboptimization The process of settling for a compromise position which is less than one would ideally need or want. See also SATISFICING.

suggestion scheme Any scheme which encourages the employees of an ORGANIZATION to suggest ways of improving the organization's operations in, for example, HEALTH AND SAFETY AT WORK, PRODUCTIVITY or QUALITY. A monetary REWARD is usually given for suggestions that are accepted. However, only the Japanese seem to take suggestion schemes seriously and one way they have formalized it is in the technique of QUALITY CIRCLES.

superego Latin for 'over I'. According to Freud the superego is one of the three main aspects of the PERSONALITY (along with the EGO and ID). Like the id with which it is always in CONFLICT, the superego is basically UNCONSCIOUS. It is the internalization of restrictions on the impulses of the id, as reflected in the values and standards of behaviour required by society in general and parents in particular. It is the equivalent of a conscience in a SYSTEM of ethics.

supernumary Someone who is surplus to requirements for an ORGANIZATION at a given time and place, e.g. as a result of OVER-MANNING.

superordinate goal In SOCIAL PSYCHOLOGY this term is used to denote a GOAL which is beyond the capacity of any one GROUP by itself to achieve and requires the active co-operation of more than one group. It is regarded as a means of promoting good relations between groups. A form of SYNERGY. See also SYNDICATE.

supervisor Anyone who supervises the work of others, although a supervisor, like a FOREMAN, is usually regarded as being on the first level of LINE MANAGEMENT in the HIERARCHY of an ORGANIZATION.

supply-side economics A form of economic policy that emphasizes the importance of supply rather than demand in the workings of the economy. It encourages measures like the removal of RESTRICTIVE PRACTICES, the reduction of the PUBLIC SECTOR in favour of the PRIVATE SECTOR and the cutting of TAXATION as an INCENTIVE to the ENTREPRENEUR. During the 1980s this policy was closely associated with the governments of Ronald Reagan in the United States and Margaret Thatcher in the United Kingdom.

survey research A technique for gathering data from large numbers of people by the use of QUESTIONNAIRES and using statistical SAMPLING methods.

sweatshop A small factory where workers are employed, who are not members of a TRADE UNION, for low PAY in harsh conditions of EMPLOYMENT. See also SUPPLY SIDE ECONOMICS.

swing shift A flexible form of SHIFT WORK practice where a shift has no set hours. The workers have a variable number of hours at WORK, depending on the circumstances, in order to ensure the continuity of PRODUCTION.

symbolic interaction This term describes a sociological method of approaching the study of SOCIAL PSYCHOLOGY. It emphasizes the part played by language, gestures and other symbols of SOCIAL INTERACTION in our conscious attempts to form ourselves and our world, and it regards our human qualities as the products of that social interaction.

sympathy The ABILITY to feel with someone. It is an emotional experience as compared to EMPATHY.

syndicate A GROUP of individuals or ORGANIZATIONS who combine for some common GOAL which is to their mutual benefit.

synectics A more narrowly-focused form of BRAINSTORMING.

synergy A situation in which the co-operation of two or more individuals, GROUPS or ORGANIZATIONS produces a combined effect which is greater than could have been produced by the sum of the separate entities, e.g. a SUPERORDINATE GOAL achieved by two groups. See also SYNDICATE.

system Any series of interconnected elements forming an organized or organic whole with a common objective. Examples can range from an individual central nervous system to a society's family and kinship arrangements.

System 4 A classification of MANAGEMENT STYLE by the American psychologist RENSIS LIKERT. There are four styles in all ranging from the autocratic (System 1) to the democratic (System 4).

systems analysis The analysis (usually by COMPUTER) of a physical SYSTEM within an ORGANIZATION, like its COMMUNICATION or heating, to see how it might be made more efficient.

systems theory The attempt to formulate general principles that could be applied to any SYSTEM by a comparative analysis of the structures and functions of as wide a variety of systems as possible.

T

T-group A form of SENSITIVITY TRAINING.

T-test In STATISTICS this is a technique for deciding whether the MEANS of two sets of scores are significantly different.

TA See TRANSACTIONAL ANALYSIS.

taboo In ANTHROPOLOGY this term is used to describe behaviour that is forbidden by a given CULTURE. It usually has magical or religious associations but is also used in a wider context for any important social prohibition. In PSYCHOANALYSIS it often refers to the REPRESSION of socially unacceptable sexual impulses, like incest.

take-over The gaining of CONTROL by one ORGANIZATION over another.

tall organization An ORGANIZATION with relatively numerous levels in its HIERARCHY. The classic examples are the army and the Civil Service with a dozen levels or more. Compare with FLAT ORGANIZATION. (Fig. 19)

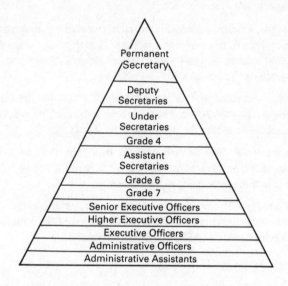

Figure 19 Tall organization (the Civil Service)

task The major element of WORK that makes up a JOB. Each task in a JOB DESCRIPTION is intended to contribute to the overall objective of the job.

task analysis The analysis of a TASK into its constituent operations for the purposes of identifying the SKILLS involved and the TRAINING necessary to improve them.

task force A GROUP of people who are brought together for a particular TASK, usually involving a special project or unusual problem. The group is normally disbanded when the task has been successfully completed.

task identity The extent to which a TASK is composed of a single, whole and identifiable piece of WORK.

task leader The individual who may emerge in a small GROUP as the person who tries to keep the attention of the group focused on its TASK and who tries to ensure that it gets done. Compare with SOCIAL-EMOTIONAL LEADER.

TAT See THEMATIC APPERCEPTION TEST.

Tavistock approach The approach to MANAGEMENT of the Tavistock Institute for Human Relations in London. See SOCIO-TECHNICAL SYSTEM and ERIC TRIST.

tax avoidance The legal attempt to reduce the burden of TAXATION on an individual or ORGANIZATION.

tax-deductible Any business expense that can be deducted from INCOME before the calculation of tax due.

tax evasion The illegal attempt to reduce the burden of TAXATION on an individual or ORGANIZATION.

taxation The levying of compulsory charges on certain items by government, as a way of raising revenue for public services, and paid by individuals and ORGANIZATIONS. These charges may be in the form of DIRECT TAXATION or INDIRECT TAXATION.

Taylor, F W (1856–1915) An American engineer who invented WORK STUDY and founded the SCIENTIFIC MANAGEMENT approach to the world of WORK (sometimes known as TAYLORISM) at the beginning of the twentieth century. He placed great emphasis on analysing the constituent operations of a TASK down to the finest details. Taylor also saw the importance of good SELECTION and TRAINING procedures and argued for better COMMUNICATION between MANAGEMENT and the SHOP FLOOR and better cooperation in general between both sides of industry.

Taylorism An alternative name for the SCIENTIFIC MANAGEMENT approach to the world of WORK pioneered by F W TAYLOR.

teaching company A business ORGANIZATION, usually in the manufacturing field, which provides students with education and TRAINING to degree standard.

teaching machine An instrument for aiding PROGRAMMED LEARNING.

team briefing The practice of encouraging COMMUNICATION in an ORGANIZATION via the FACE-TO-FACE GROUP.

team-building A technique that aims to help WORK GROUPS by improving the QUALITY of their members' INTERPERSONAL RELATIONS as well as their SKILL at solving problems and accomplishing their TASK. This is usually done with the aid of an external CONSULTANCY which will diagnose the way the work group functions, helping members to identify difficulties and suggest improvements.

technological change Industrial and social change, leading to changes in the workplace ENVIRONMENT, which can be attributed to the introduction of TECHNOLOGY.

technological unemployment UNEMPLOYMENT that can be attributed directly to the introduction of a particular TECHNOLOGY to the workplace.

technology The practical application of scientific innovation to industry.

technology transfer The transfer of a TECHNOLOGY from an area in which it has been successfully applied to an area in which it has not yet been tried.

telecommunications Any form of COMMUNICATION by electronic means.

teleconference A discussion or conference where participants are geographically scattered and linked by means of TELECOMMUNICATION such as AUDIOCONFERENCING or VIDEOCONFERENCING.

telephone interviewing An adaptation of the INTERVIEW technique used in SURVEY RESEARCH where face-to-face interviewing is not possible or advisable.

teleworking The application of TELECOMMUNICATIONS to benefit the HOME-WORKER and to encourage other people to WORK from home.

test Any procedure for the ASSESSMENT of a specific ABILITY or APTITUDE or psychological state. See also PSYCHOLOGICAL TEST.

test marketing A form of PILOT STUDY on a new product, where it is tried out in a limited area first in order to see whether it would be worth MARKETING more widely.

Thematic Apperception Test A PROJECTIVE TECHNIQUE developed in the late 1930s by the American psychologist Henry Murray. It consists of vague and ambiguous drawings (usually of one or two human figures) about each of which the subject has to make up a story. The themes that may emerge from these stories are then used to diagnose areas of emotional CONFLICT or concern in the subject. This technique has been widely used in the SELECTION of SENIOR MANAGEMENT where, for example, the incidence of ACHIEVEMENT imagery might be of particular interest.

Theory X In the terminology of DOUGLAS McGREGOR this describes the RATIONAL-ECONOMIC view of human nature that people only WORK when they have to and therefore require AUTHORITARIAN MANAGEMENT. McGregor rejected this view in favour of THEORY Y.

Theory Y In the terminology of DOUGLAS McGREGOR this describes a view of human nature in which people whould like to be creative in their WORK and take more responsibility for it. They would thus be more responsive to DEMOCRATIC MANAGEMENT and its enabling function than is suggested by the proponents of THEORY X.

Theory Z The term suggested by the American writer on ORGANIZATIONAL THEORY William Ouchi for western adaptations of Japanese MANAGEMENT practices. The Theory Z ORGANIZATION is distinguished by several important features: 1 lifetime EMPLOYMENT; 2 relatively slow PROMOTION; 3 concern for the whole person; 4 informal CONTROL and LEADERSHIP; 5 individual responsibility; 6 consensual decision-making; 7 relatively less SPECIALIZATION. There is some evidence that Theory Z organizations have less ABSENTEEISM, greater PRODUCTIVITY and better QUALITY output than others.

therapy See PSYCHOTHERAPY.

therblig A term used in the WORK STUDY area of ERGONOMICS. It is an anagram of its inventor's name, GILBRETH. A therblig is one of eighteen fundamental operations in a worker's activities. Therbligs are used in conjunction with a SIMO CHART and each has a symbol that describes the bodily movements involved, like 'hold' or 'select'. (Fig. 20)

third force A term used in PSYCHOLOGY to describe those psychologists who subscribe to a view of the human condition based neither on BEHAVIOURISM nor on PSYCHOANALYSIS, but one based broadly on HUMANISTIC PSYCHOLOGY.

threshold In ERGONOMICS this term describes two ways of indicating sensitivity to sensory stimulation. The *absolute threshold* is the minimum amount of stimulation necessary for the subject to detect it. The *differential threshold* is the minimum change in stimulation necessary to produce a JUST NOTICEABLE DIFFERENCE.

throughput The amount of material that goes through the entire process of PRODUCTION in a given time.

time-and-a-half A form of OVERTIME working in which time worked is paid at one-and-a-half times the normal rate.

Symbol	Name	Colour coding
⌔	search	black
⌖	find	grey
 →	select	light grey
∩	grasp	red
⌓	hold	gold ochre
⌣	transport load	green
9	position	blue
#	assemble	violet
∪	use	purple
⫟	disassemble	light violet
0	inspect	burnt ochre
⚲	pre-position	pale blue
⌢	release load	carmine red
⌣	transport empty	olive green
ℇ	rest for overcoming fatigue	orange
⌂	unavoidable delay	yellow
⌐ₒ	avoidable delay	lemon yellow
℗	plan	brown

Figure 20 Therbligs

time-and-motion study See WORK STUDY.

time budget The preparation of a detailed timetable of WORK activities in order to help improve time MANAGEMENT and efficiency.

time horizon The degree to which the PLANNING of an ORGANIZATION or an individual MANAGER extends into the future.

time in lieu A period of time off WORK, usually taken at the employee's discretion, to make up for time worked over and above normal working hours, i.e. an exchange of time for the money that would have been paid for working an OVERTIME rate.

time sharing   A situation in which two or more people or ORGANIZ-ATIONS make use of the same piece of equipment (particularly a COMPUTER) in order to share costs and to maximize use of the resource.

time-span of discretion   A term introduced to the WORK STUDY area of ERGONOMICS in the 1960s by the British industrial psychologist Elliott Jaques. It is an attempt at EQUITY in setting salary levels and DIFFER-ENTIALS following a JOB EVALUATION. What is measured is the length of time during which someone has to exercise discretion, i.e. personal judgement and responsibility, in their JOB before requiring decisions from superiors.

tm   See TRADE MARK.

tokenism   An action taken for its symbolic value as opposed to a serious attempt at changing a given situation, e.g., appointing a lone woman to an all-male board of directors as an end in itself, i.e. to show how open-minded and progressive the ORGANIZATION is.

tolerance for ambiguity   The ABILITY to live with a situation that is not clear cut, where different interpretations of what is happening are possible and where the outlook is obscure; in sum, the ability to accept complexity in human affairs without seeking the comfort of simplistic solutions. In PSYCHOLOGY, high tolerance for ambiguity is usually seen as a sign of psychological health and maturity.

total quality   An approach to, and concern for, QUALITY which pervades the ORGANIZATION from top to bottom. It was originally introduced to Japan in the aftermath of the Second World War by the American engineers W Edwards Deming and Joseph Duran. It is based on close attention to detail, self-monitoring by workers at each step and a passionate commitment to quality as part of an organization's IDENTITY, and which is internalized by everyone in it. This approach is customer-driven and aims for ZERO DEFECTS, while being imbued with the spirit of KAIZEN or continuous improvement.

tracking   In ERGONOMICS this term refers to the SKILL of an individual in making the necessary adjustments of hand and eye to follow a moving object in a visual display.

trade association   A voluntary grouping of ORGANIZATIONS in the same business which combine for mutual benefit, e.g. in trying to influence government legislation. See also EMPLOYERS' ASSOCIATION.

trade mark Any form of LOGO and/or wording which a company uses to identify its products or BRANDS and distinguish them from their rivals. Like a COPYRIGHT or a PATENT, the owner of a trade mark which has been officially registered has the MONOPOLY right to use it for a certain period of time.

trade press Journals, magazines or newspapers that cater for the interests of a particular trade or industry.

trade secret Information or techniques known only to members of a particular trade or PROFESSION, public knowledge of which would detract from their standing and INCOME, e.g. how a magician saws a lady in half.

trade union An ORGANIZATION of workers in a particular trade or industry which furthers the welfare of its members and acts on their behalf in COLLECTIVE BARGAINING with employers on PAY and conditions of EMPLOYMENT.

tradition-directed A term introduced to SOCIOLOGY in the United States in the 1950s by David Riesman to describe people who interact with their society mainly by following the rules and customs laid down in its traditions. See also INNER-DIRECTED and OUTER-DIRECTED.

training An area of PERSONNEL MANAGEMENT concerned with making the best use of the HUMAN RESOURCES in an ORGANIZATION by providing them with the appropriate instruction to acquire the necessary SKILLS for their JOBS. See also GROUP TRAINING METHODS, MANAGEMENT DEVELOPMENT and TEAM-BUILDING.

trait Any enduring characteristic of an individual's PERSONALITY.

trait theory Any approach to the study of LEADERSHIP which emphasizes the importance of trying to identify distinguishing characteristics or TRAITS of PERSONALITY common to successful leaders.

transactional analysis A form of GROUP THERAPY in which the interrelationships of the GROUP members are analysed in terms of their transactions with each other in the ROLE of 'parent', 'child', or 'adult' (their EGO states in TA language). Transactional Analysis was developed in the 1960s by the American psychiatrist Eric Berne.

transactional leadership A term introduced into the study of LEADERSHIP in the 1960s by the British political scientist Tom Burns to describe a MANAGER in an ORGANIZATION who is more concerned with the means of achieving the organization's ends or GOALS than in the nature of these ends. Burns considered this type of leadership essential for the efficient day-to-day running of the organization and the continuing MOTIVATION of the work-force. See also TRANSFORMATIONAL LEADERSHIP, with which it is always contrasted.

transfer of training The process whereby the LEARNING achieved in one situation is transferred to another situation. This can have positive effects (knowing Spanish aids the learning of Italian) or sometimes negative effects (knowing how to steer a car is detrimental to steering a boat with a tiller). See also LEARNING SET.

transformational leadership A term introduced into the study of LEADERSHIP in the 1960s by the British political scientist Tom Burns to describe a MANAGER in an ORGANIZATION who is more concerned with the nature of the ends or GOALS of an ORGANIZATION than in the means of achieving them. Burns considered this type of leadership essential in reassessing the organization's goals and values and the direction in which it is going as well as the EMPOWERMENT of the work-force to be creative in their JOBS. See also TRANSACTIONAL LEADERSHIP with which it is always contrasted.

travel-to-work area The geographical area over which people are willing to commute daily to WORK in a given ORGANIZATION.

trial and error learning The step-by-step form of LEARNING, over many trials, characteristic of most animal learning and much human learning, and the basis for CONDITIONING procedures. It is a very laborious process compared to INSIGHT LEARNING.

Trist, Eric A leading British industrial sociologist concerned with GROUP WORKING practices who developed the concept of the SOCIO-TECHNICAL SYSTEM.

trust-control dilemma The basic problem of DELEGATION faced, at any level, by a MANAGER in an ORGANIZATION of how much trust to have in the subordinate to whom the WORK is delegated and how much CONTROL, if any, of the work to retain.

turnover 1 The amount of sales revenue achieved or business transacted during a given period of time. 2 Loss of people from, and appointments to, the work-force during a given period of time. 3 The THROUGHPUT of stock in either manufacturing PRODUCTION or in services.

two-factor theory See HERZBERG TWO-FACTOR THEORY.

two-step flow of communication The idea that the MASS MEDIA of COMMUNICATION first influence the OPINION LEADERS in a community who in turn influence the opinions and ATTITUDES of others.

Type A personality A set of PERSONALITY characteristics that have been linked to a particular susceptibility to heart disease. These characteristics include being impatient, always rushing, trying to do too many things at once, walking, talking and eating fast, being hard-driving at WORK, having few interests outside work and hiding feelings. Type A personality is always contrasted with TYPE B PERSONALITY.

Type B personality A set of PERSONALITY characteristics that are the opposite of TYPE A PERSONALITY and therefore considered to be much less susceptible to heart disease. These characteristics include being casual about appointments, being a good listener, never feeling rushed, slow and deliberate in manner and speech, easy-going, many interests outside WORK and able to express feelings. Both Types A and B are extreme instances and people would generally fall somewhere between the two.

typing Dealing with people as STEREOTYPES.

U

unconscious This is the most important concept in PSYCHOANALYSIS. It is the region of the psyche that contains impulses and desires whch are too threatening to be allowed into consciousness and from which they have been repressed or inhibited from entering. The effects of this REPRESSION and INHIBITION are expressed in consciousness as disturbed behaviour. While FREUD did not discover the unconscious (and never claimed to have done so), he systematically probed the dynamic mechanisms involved in its relationship with the conscious psyche, and did more than anyone else to expose the great amount of irrationality in human affairs.

unconscious ideology An IDEOLOGY which underlies and guides someone's behaviour but of which they are not consciously aware.

unconscious motivation Any MOTIVATION of whose origin, or even existence, a person is not consciously aware.

underachiever A person who fails to meet the level of ACHIEVEMENT expected of her. This term is sometimes used in the field of education to describe someone who doesn't try hard enough, i.e. a person whose ABILITY could take her beyond her ambitions. Contrast with OVERACHIEVER.

underemployment A situation in which people do not have enough WORK to do or are not being fully utilized in terms of their SKILL level.

undermanning A situation in which there are fewer people employed by an ORGANIZATION than are necessary for the efficient PERFORMANCE of its WORK. Compare with OVERMANNING.

unemployment The term generally used of people who are able and willing to engage in paid EMPLOYMENT but unable to find any. See also SEASONAL UNEMPLOYMENT, STRUCTURAL UNEMPLOYMENT and TECHNOLOGICAL UNEMPLOYMENT. The exact definition of unemployment is a matter of some political contention.

unfair dismissal The verdict of an INDUSTRIAL TRIBUNAL which is sought by an employee who feels he has been wrongfully dismissed by his employer. The employer has to show that the dismissal was fair and legal. See also CONSTRUCTIVE DISMISSAL.

union See TRADE UNION.

unique selling point In MARKETING, this term refers to the distinctive feature of a product that gives it a COMPETITIVE ADVANTAGE.

unit cost The cost of one unit of PRODUCTION or of a single item. It is found by dividing the total costs by the number of units or items produced.

unity of command In ORGANIZATIONAL THEORY, this is the principle that each member of an ORGANIZATION should report to only one person. See also AUTHORITY and FUNCTIONAL AUTHORITY.

unstructured interview An INTERVIEW which is not guided by a set of fixed questions, or perhaps even topics, from the interviewer but in which as free and open a discussion as possible is encouraged within the constraints of time and the objective of the interview. This method emphasizes flexibility for the interviewer and scope for expression by the interviewee, at the expense of comparability across respondents. In practice most interviews of whatever kind fall somewhere between the completely unstructured interview and the totally STRUCTURED INTERVIEW.

upward communication COMMUNICATION from lower levels of employees up to SENIOR MANAGEMENT in the HIERARCHY of an ORGANIZATION. A much more difficult proposition than either DOWNWARD COMMUNICATION or HORIZONTAL COMMUNICATION.

user friendly A product, especially in the COMPUTER world, in which the needs and convenience of the potential user have been fully considered. See also TOTAL QUALITY.

USP See UNIQUE SELLING POINT.

utility 1 In ECONOMICS, the term implies the usefulness or satisfaction to be derived from a product by a potential buyer. 2 Something that performs a useful service, like a PUBLIC UTILITY.

V

value added See ADDED VALUE.

value for money A term used, particularly in the PUBLIC SECTOR, to denote the benefit derived from a particular expenditure for a particular purpose.

variance In STATISTICS this is the square of the STANDARD DEVIATION. It is used to measure the spread of scores in a particular TEST or experiment.

VDU See VISUAL DISPLAY UNIT.

venture capital See RISK CAPITAL.

vertical communication A term sometimes applied to DOWNWARD COMMUNICATION, though more usually to UPWARD COMMUNICATION in an ORGANIZATION.

vertical integration The process whereby a company extends its business interests into other stages of PRODUCTION of, or sales of, its products. Though sometimes a company is able to do this for itself, it is usually accomplished by some form of MERGER with, or TAKEOVER of, another firm concerned with a different stage of the same product, e.g. a publisher may take over a bookshop. Compare with HORIZONTAL INTEGRATION.

VFM See VALUE FOR MONEY.

victimization The persistently unfair treatment of a worker, either by colleagues or employers. See also SCAPEGOATING.

videoconferencing A TELECONFERENCE using video, as well as audio, means of COMMUNICATION.

visual display unit The part of a COMPUTER that provides a visual display of its operations on a television-like screen.

visual search In ERGONOMICS, this term refers to the process of scanning a set of instruments or CONTROLS for relevant information.

vocational guidance A branch of OCCUPATIONAL PSYCHOLOGY which helps people to choose an occupation or a career which will be of mutual benefit to them and their prospective employers. It makes use of the INTERVIEW technique plus an extensive battery of PSYCHOLOGICAL TESTS, including tests of ABILITY, APTITUDE and NEED FOR ACHIEVEMENT.

voluntary redundancy A situation in which an employee requests or agrees to REDUNDANCY, usually in return for favourable terms of compensation.

voluntary work Unpaid WORK done by volunteers for a charity or similar ORGANIZATION.

Vroom-Yetton model A CONTINGENCY THEORY OF LEADERSHIP that uses a DECISION TREE to identify the most appropriate LEADERSHIP STYLE for a given situation. It was developed by two American industrial psychologists, Vroom and Yetton.

W

wage differentials See DIFFERENTIALS.

wastage See NATURAL WASTAGE.

wasting assets ASSETS whose economic value decreases as they are used because they cannot practically be renewed or replaced, e.g. coal-mines or oilfields.

Watson, J B (1878–1958) An American psychologist, and later ADVERTISING EXECUTIVE, who is generally regarded as the father of BEHAVIOURISM.

welfare function The basic function of PERSONNEL MANAGEMENT which implies responsibility for the well-being of an organization's members, physical, mental and social. At the very least this will include HEALTH AND SAFETY AT WORK but, depending on the policy of the ORGANIZATION, it may also include many other things, like AFFIRMATIVE ACTION, PATERNITY LEAVE, or the provision of a crèche for working mothers of small children.

welfare state A country whose government accepts that it has the primary responsibility to look after the welfare of its citizens; their education, health, EMPLOYMENT and RETIREMENT in particular.

whistle blowing The public exposure of corrupt, illegal, or unethical practices by an ORGANIZATION, usually on the part of an individual member though sometimes by a body responsible for overseeing the organization which lacks the AUTHORITY or POWER to impose penalties for wrongdoing.

white-collar crime Criminal offences associated with businessmen or WHITE-COLLAR WORKERS, like embezzlement, fraud or insider dealing on the stock MARKET.

white-collar worker Popular term for any member of STAFF who works in an office. The name derives from the practice of (men) wearing a white shirt to WORK (in the days when men wore white shirts – with white collars). Usually contrasted with a BLUE-COLLAR WORKER.

whole method A technique for LEARNING in which the material is learned as a whole on each PRACTICE or repetition. Compare this with the PART METHOD.

wholesaling Acting as an intermediary or MIDDLEMAN between the PRODUCTION of goods and their RETAILING to the general public. It usually involves the stocking of relatively large quantities of goods for onward DISTRIBUTION.

widget A NEOLOGISM which is sometimes used in discussions of MARKETING or PRODUCTION to refer to a generalized standard item rather than a specific product.

wildcat strike A local STRIKE that does not have official TRADE UNION backing, usually called without warning or at short notice.

windfall profit An unexpected PROFIT, usually arising from matters not directly connected with the activities of the lucky individual or

ORGANIZATION, e.g. a bequest, or a change in TAXATION. The original 'windfall' consisted of apples blown off trees.

word-of-mouth marketing   A form of MARKETING for goods or services whose ADVERTISING is based on personal recommendation, e.g. finding a plumber or a lawyer.

word processor   A MICROCOMPUTER, used only for the word processing functions of typing and editing, which has taken over from the typewriter in the modern ELECTRONIC OFFICE. It consists of a keyboard and a VISUAL DISPLAY UNIT and usually has a printer attached to produce HARD COPY. It works from text stored on FLOPPY DISKS.

work   Any kind of purposive activity whether paid or unpaid, full-time or part-time, formal or informal. With reference to an ORGANIZATION it is used about the operations involved in a particular JOB or TASK.

work design   The part of the JOB DESIGN process that is concerned with the actual working operations, as opposed to the PERSONNEL MANAGEMENT aspects.

work ethic   See PROTESTANT WORK ETHIC.

work experience   A period of time spent doing unpaid WORK in a workplace ENVIRONMENT by young people about to leave school, as preparation for future EMPLOYMENT.

work flow   The arrangement of JOBS in a particular sequence intended to help an ORGANIZATION run smoothly and productively.

work group   A GROUP of people engaged in doing some WORK together who are also linked by INTERPERSONAL RELATIONS which are important to them.

work measurement   An integral part of the WORK STUDY process in which a variety of (subjective) methods, like WORK SAMPLING, are used to fix a standard time for the acceptable PERFORMANCE of a given TASK by a trained worker.

work organization   Any ORGANIZATION which, in the course of trying to fulfil its GOALS, gives paid EMPLOYMENT (whether full-time or part-time) to one or more workers.

work role   See ROLE.

work sampling   A technique used in WORK MEASUREMENT and WORK STUDY for obtaining information about a particular JOB or TASK by the process of SAMPLING (usually RANDOM SAMPLING) from the WORK activities at various times rather than by continuous observation.

work simplification   A process used in ORGANIZATION AND METHODS or WORK STUDY where a SYSTEM of WORK is examined to see if unnecessary expenditure of energy can be removed. Compare with JOB SIMPLIFICATION.

work study   A set of techniques, including WORK MEASUREMENT, which analyse a given area of WORK to see whether PERFORMANCE can be made more efficient and economical. It is based on the SCIENTIFIC MANAGEMENT approach to the study of the ORGANIZATION.

work-to-rule   A form of INDUSTRIAL ACTION, short of a STRIKE, where workers do not withdraw their labour but any co-operation with their employers, beyond the explicit contractual agreement made for them by their TRADE UNION. The net effect on the ORGANIZATION is usually the same as a GO-SLOW, and they are often used together. One effect of these actions is to expose the degree to which the organization in question depends upon the unwritten co-operation and GOODWILL of its employees.

workaholic   Someone who uses WORK the way an alcoholic uses alcohol, as a way of trying to escape from their personal problems.

worker-director   A representative of the work-force on the board of directors of an ORGANIZATION. This is sometimes considered the ultimate in INDUSTRIAL DEMOCRACY. It is extremely rare.

works council   A forum for JOINT CONSULTATION between employees and employers (or their representatives) in an ORGANIZATION.

workstation   The physical ENVIRONMENT in which a JOB is done. It is used most often to refer to the location of a COMPUTER operator or WORD PROCESSOR operator.

WP   See WORD PROCESSOR.

Z

Zeigarnik effect   A finding by a GESTALT psychologist named Bluma Zeigarnik that subjects are more likely to remember details of TASKS during which they were interrupted than those they were allowed to complete. The effect has been claimed for many situations where someone is interrupted.

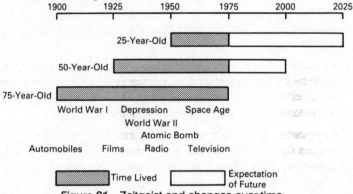

Figure 21 Zeitgeist and changes over time

zeitgeist A German term meaning literally 'spirit of the times'. It is used to denote the prevailing social and political mood of an era, the conventional wisdom, the fads and fashions in everything from hair length to PSYCHOLOGY. A zeitgeist affects the emotional and mental life of everyone who lives through it, and is thought to have similar effects on people of a similar age GROUP, thus providing one basis for generational differences. (Fig. 21)

zero-based budgeting The use of BUDGETS which start from a present base of zero and regard all future expenditure as being on new items rather than a continuation of existing ones. In practice this means that a budget has to be justified in full for each year of operation.

zero defects The objective of a policy of TOTAL QUALITY. It is to have every single item produced and delivered to the customer completely perfect, as opposed to working within an acceptable range of QUALITY, and therefore defectiveness.

zero-sum game In GAME THEORY this is a situation where one person's losses are another's gains because there is a finite amount to be won, i.e. the gains and losses in the game add up to zero. This situation has been suggested as a MODEL for many people of the DISTRIBUTION of REWARDS in society.